Chicken Little

Marie-Louise von Franz, Honorary Patron

**Studies in Jungian Psychology
by Jungian Analysts**

Daryl Sharp, General Editor

CHICKEN LITTLE
The Inside Story

A Jungian Romance

Daryl Sharp

For Fraser

Canadian Cataloguing in Publication Data

Sharp, Daryl, 1936-
    Chicken Little: the inside story (a Jungian romance)

(Studies in Jungian psychology by Jungian analysts; 61)

Includes bibliographical references.

ISBN 0-919123-62-7

1. Chicken Licken.
2. Symbolism in folk literature—Psychological aspects.
3. Individuation (Psychology).
4. Jung, C.G. (Carl Gustav), 1875-1961.
I. Title.   II. Series.

GR735.S53 1993   398.24'528617   C93-093601-9

INNER CITY BOOKS
Box 1271, Station Q, Toronto, Canada M4T 2P4
Telephone (416) 927-0355
FAX 416-924-1814

Honorary Patron: Marie-Louise von Franz.
Publisher and General Editor: Daryl Sharp.
Senior Editor: Victoria Cowan.

INNER CITY BOOKS was founded in 1980 to promote the
understanding and practical application of the work of C.G. Jung.

Cover painting by Jessy-Kate Cowan-Sharp

Printed and bound in Canada by John Deyell Company

Contents

Chicken Little:
Messiah, Meshuggeneh or Metaphor?*

"The sky is falling!" cried Chicken Little. "The sky is falling!"—and everywhere she went people laughed. They had known the gloom and doom of recession, depression, inflation, deflation, stagflation and so on. They saw recovery in sight and were ready for a joke.

But Chicken Little wasn't interested in economics. She was concerned with the imminent collapse of the heavens. The survival of the monetary system was not her business. Her apocalyptic vision was much grander than that. Indeed, today some see her as the first environmentalist.

"The sky is falling!" cried Chicken Little. A simple declarative sentence: article, noun, verb, gerund. And everybody laughed.

Now, that's not literally true. A few feathered friends took her words at face value (giving rise to the popular "mass mania" theory) but in the end they shared her fate. Like the hapless Cassandra in Greek mythology—blessed by Apollo with the gift of prophecy and then cursed by him because she spurned his patriarchal embrace—Chicken Little was saddled with the foreknowledge that whatever she said would not be believed.[1]

Some commentators believe that Freud's pioneering work *Studies in Hysteria* is a thinly veiled analysis of Chicken Little. Others aren't so sure. C.G. Jung, in a long essay championing the inner voice, wrote:

> The individual will never find the real justification for [her] existence and [her] own spiritual and moral autonomy anywhere except in an extramundane principle capable of relativizing the overpowering influence of external factors. The individual who is not anchored in God can offer no resistance on [her] own resources to the physical and moral blandishments of the world. For this [she] needs the evi-

---

* Meshuggeneh is a Yiddish expression for crazy person.
[1] For a clinical study of this syndrome, see Laurie Layton Schapira, *The Cassandra Complex: Living with Disbelief.*

dence of inner, transcendent experience which alone can protect [her] from the otherwise inevitable submersion in the mass.[2]

Did Chicken Little feel the hand of God, then? Was her shrill warning really an apotropaic attempt to protect herself against the mass? We don't know. Only one thing is sure: Chicken Little could not contain herself. Believed or not, she had to speak out, that was her destiny. Which is to say, she did what she had to do.

To my mind she is a perfect example—perhaps even the original model—of the woman M. Esther Harding describes as "one-in-herself":

> The woman who is virgin, one-in-herself, does what she does, not because of any desire to please, not to be liked, or to be approved, even by herself; not because of any desire to gain power over another, to catch his interest or love, but because what she does is true.[3]

The heart-wrenching saga of Chicken Little, like the heroic epic of Gilgamesh and Enkidu, has been passed down from generation to generation. No one knows exactly how old it is. It first surfaced some three hundred years ago on seven stone tablets discovered in Lower Kraznac, deep in the Carpathian Mountains, by a traveling monk looking for succor. Some tablets are whole, others are merely fragments. There are huge gaps. The first seems to start in mid-story, and the seventh ends so abruptly that one cannot help but think that others are still to be found.

It took 73 years to decipher the Kraznac tablets—three generations of astute hermetic linguists working 10 hours a day, 7 days a week, 365 days a year. Indeed, their labors have been aptly compared with the construction of the pyramids, medieval cathedrals and the Great Wall of China. It is true that modern Chicken Little scholars dispute some of their interpretations, but all honor is due these diligent pioneers, for they did lay the groundwork and gave us indisputably rich insights into the fowl psyche.

---

[2] "The Undiscovered Self," *Civilization in Transition*, CW 10, par. 511.

[3] *Woman's Mysteries: Ancient and Modern*, p. 147. This theme is further developed in Marion Woodman, *The Pregnant Virgin: A Process of Psychological Transformation*.

An alchemical scribe by the code name of Marcus Marcianus recorded Chicken Little's vision, albeit disguised and with a rather optimistic hue, on a medieval illuminated manuscript:

> Heaven above,
> Heaven below.
> Stars above,
> Stars below.
> All that is above
> Also is below.
> Grasp this and rejoice.

That memorable gem came to light in a French count's library in 1745. It subsequently passed through many hands and was auctioned off in London by Sotheby's as recently as 1983. Jung himself quotes it in "The Psychology of the Transference,"[4] though he fails to track its source back to Chicken Little. It is also cited in Marie-Louise von Franz's classic, *Puer Aeternus,* where she uses it as a stepping stone for all sorts of arcane speculations, like interpreting the stars as archetypes of the collective unconscious—nuclei, so to speak, in the dark sky of the unconscious.[5] I am a long-standing admirer of Marie-Louise von Franz, and particularly of that book, but she too fails to acknowledge Chicken Little's seminal influence on Western culture.

Needless to say, I have a thing about Chicken Little. It goes back to when I first heard about her at the age of six. At that time I still believed in Santa Claus and the Easter bunny, and I thought God made all the houses. Those fantasies died, but my interest in Chicken Little survived.

Apparently I'm not alone. Since the tablets were unearthed, Chicken Little's story has been told and retold many times, often with variations but always in the vernacular. At last count, I have personally read thirty-seven versions. The details often differ but the essentials are the same.

I've also read pretty well all the Chicken Little scholarship—Chickle Schtick, as we call it—and I've been privileged to examine

---

[4] *The Practice of Psychotherapy,* CW 16, par. 384.
[5] *Puer Aeternus,* p. 143.

authenticated replicas of the Kraznac tablets. To me, the definitive study is still Adam Brillig's essay, "A Non-Euclidean Perspective on Ms. Little."[6] Professor Brillig, a Zürich-trained analyst, is a well-known Chickle Schticker. To my knowledge he was the first to ponder in print whether the modifying monicker "Little" was sexist. Why not Chicken Big? he asked. Denigration of the feminine, he pointed out, has long been rife in the patriarchal West and it would be no surprise to find it in the barnyard.

I shall often refer to Brillig's views in this paper, for they have a patina of psychological truth, buttressed by personal experience, that is hard to refute.

Chicken Little's story is simple enough, at least on the surface. I shall tell it now, interspersed with my own observations.[7]

> Chicken Little was on her way through the woods to her grandmother's when something fell on her head. She picked herself up and shrieked, "The sky is falling!" Then she gathered her skirts and ran off in all directions. "Help! The sky is falling!" she cried. "Help! Help! The sky is falling!"

I have mentioned variations. There's an Indian tale where the impending apocalypse is announced by a hare. In Sri Lanka a bat gets the nod, in Borneo a mongoose, in Australia a bandicoot.

Stephen Kellogg's well-known illustrated version actually begins not with Chicken Little but with a fox—Foxy Loxy—lurking behind a hedge. Foxy Loxy sees Chicken Little and immediately thinks of supper. The fragmentary line giving rise to this possibility, on the first broken tablet, is traditionally read as ". . . eat her up."

Of course, Kellogg's telling is also based on the known fact that foxes are natural predators of chickens, but Adam Brillig gives short shrift to his interpretation. After a devastating attack on Kellogg's academic credentials, he asks:

> Why "up"? "Down" would make more sense. Chicken Little was a bird, after all.[8]

---

[6] *Journal of Forensic Ethnology,* vol. 12, no. 2 (1968), pp. 24-46.

[7] For the purpose of this paper I have focused on the bare-bones story that unfolds in the Kraznac tablets. Sorting out complex from archetype in modern versions can drive one mad.

[8] "A Non-Euclidean Perspective," op. cit., p. 29.

Now doesn't that echo the old alchemical saying, "All that is above also is below"? Brillig continues:

> If we accept the word "up" here, we are in all honor driven to inquire, as some already have, whether it is to be taken as an adverb or a noun. If the latter, we are obliged to ask which part of the body it refers to. I can only compare it to the old oxymoron journalism students are alerted to—"A police spokesman said Ms. X was shot at close quarters and the bullet is in her yet."
>
> Only in Chinese acupuncture is any part of the human anatomy designated as "yet," namely a tiny bone in the inner ear. Although the time frame of the Kraznac tablets doesn't entirely negate this correspondence, it stretches one's credulity to imagine a fox licking his lips over a chicken's inner ear. Of course, we might take "up" as an early variant of, or shorthand for, "pudendum," but I suggest we escape what threatens to become a precipitous descent into absurdity by leaving Foxy Loxy out.[9]

In some accounts Chicken Little is hit by an acorn; in others by a falling coconut, a piece of ripe fruit or a branch (variously a limb from an acacia tree, an elder or a Japanese maple). One study suggests she was struck by lightning, which, in accordance with Jung's thoughts in "A Study in the Process of Individuation,"[10] would point to a strong message from the Self. Another, with weak supporting evidence, questions whether she was hit by anything at all and implies it was all in her mind (the hysteria theory). Adam Brillig accepts that Chicken Little was felled by a piece of tree (though of indeterminate flora) but questions just about everything else.

For instance, how old was Chicken Little? The tablets are quiet on this point; yes, they imply pubescence, but possibly that's a modern projection. And was her grandmother's really her destination? Perhaps it was simply a plausible excuse for being out at all. Indeed, Brillig raises the possibility—more thinkable today than twenty years ago, thanks to the recovery movement—that she was escaping abusive parents.

---

[9] Ibid.

[10] "Lightning signifies a sudden, unexpected, and overpowering change of psychic condition." *(The Archetypes and the Collective Unconscious,* CW 9i, par. 533)

The feminist Chickle Schticker Janet Marble, in an article commissioned for *Cosmopolitan,* toys with the idea that Chicken Little was on her way to a romantic assignation. She writes:

> I cut my scholarly teeth on Alice B. Toklas. A chicken is a chicken is a chicken. Red blood flows in the veins of chickens, just as it courses through ours. The entire animal world, which indisputably includes chickens, is subject to this coursing of blood and the flood of compelling desire occasioned by its wake. We cannot lightly assume that Chicken Little, alone of her genre, was immune to the forces of nature. My gut feeling tells me she was feeling her oats— hot to trot, so to speak.[11]

Marble then suggests that *if* Ms. Little was married, and *if* her mate was, pardon me, a "foul fucker," she'd have ample motive for a fling. Writes Marble:

> All power to her. I'd do the same.[12]

A.G. Grandize goes further:

> The traditional characterization of Chicken Little as "innocent" has not been proven. Indeed, what if she were pregnant? She wouldn't be the first youngster to panic at being knocked up. In which case due consideration must be given to the possibility that she was on her way to what then passed for a family planning clinic, or the local midwife, or even, in light of pre-Christian morals—though God forbid—a fetal egg plucker.[13]

Such speculations may appeal to the prurient, but to my mind they go over the top. For if Chicken Little really had a lover, who was it?

Well might one ask. As we shall see, the Kraznac tablets mention only three male presences: the pompous Turkey Lurkey (a patriarchal buzzard), the gardener Ducky Lucky (possibly gay),[14] and Gosling Gilbert (a tad).[15] Yes, subjectively they are animus figures, but does

---

[11] September, 1978, p. 168.

[12] Ibid.

[13] *American Journal of Chickle Schtick,* vol. 17, no. 3 (1964), p. 138.

[14] The authoritative work in this field is Graham Jackson, *The Secret Lore of Gardening: Patterns of Male Intimacy,* p. 103.

[15] I purposely leave out the aforementioned Foxy Loxy, Stephen Kellog's shady invention. For if Foxy Loxy, why not Rodney Rabbit? Billy Beaver?

any fit the bill as a potential sex partner? I think not. One can't entirely discount the possibility, psychologically, of a demon lover,[16] but, and more to the point, nowhere in the tablets is there a shred of evidence that Chicken Little was capable of lust. Of course, this raises the whole body issue, which I gladly leave to those more qualified.[17]

Personally, I can live with Chicken Little as unmarried, in her early teens, and the grandmother as her goal. After all, we find the same motif in Little Red Riding Hood and in Russian fairy tales (where the grandmother figure, Baba Yaga, is arguably evil). The natural process of development in women beckons, perhaps obliges, them to make contact with both positive and negative sides of the Great Mother.[18] As often as not, along the way, something hits them on the head. Goodness knows, I have no quarrel with that. What I question is the skirts.[19]

Carbon dating of the tablets places their origin between 5200 and 4800 BC. Authoritative sources point out that skirts were not even thought of at that time, and in fact were not prevalent until 1805, when to celebrate Napoleon they suddenly appeared everywhere on the streets of Paris. On this issue I definitely side with Adam Brillig. After exhaustive research he wrote the following:

> The glyph on the Kraznac tablets commonly interpreted as "skirt" is more accurately translated, at least in this context, as "shit." I do not propose this lightly, only to set the record straight. Nothing is more abhorrent to me than scholarship based on ignorance. Laymen on a day's etymological jaunt, all jovial and carefree, more concerned with self-serving twaddle than the truth, may be forgiven such gaucheries.

Willy Whippet? We might as well ignore the tablets altogether and write our own soap opera. For similar reasons I cannot take seriously the fatuous theory that Chicken Little was actually a *male transvestite,* or at best a not too fastidious cross-dresser.

[16] See Marion Woodman, *Addiction to Perfection,* pp. 135-155.

[17] See, for instance, Deldon Anne McNeely, *Touching: Body Therapy and Depth Psychology,* and Marion Woodman, *The Owl Was a Baker's Daughter: Obesity, Anorexia Nervosa and the Repressed Feminine.*

[18] See Sibylle Birkhäuser-Oeri, *The Mother: Archetypal Image in Fairy Tales.*

[19] See above, p. 10: "Then she gathered her skirts and ran off in all directions."

Genuine Chickle Schtickers have no excuse. In this light, my considered opinion is that the phrase "gathered her skirts" is more accurately translated as "got her shit together."[20]

Now there's something to get your teeth into. Make no mistake about it: Brillig's insight reveals this apparently innocuous little tale for what it really is—no less than a thinly disguised paradigm of a woman's need to integrate her shadow.

To continue with the story:

Chicken Little's cries were heard by a neighbor, Henny Penny, who asked, "What's the matter?"[21]

"The sky is falling!" cried Chicken Little. "A piece of it hit me on the head!"

Henny Penny was horrified. "Call the police!" she cried, and echoed, "The sky is falling!"

Here is the first mention of an authority figure. While the Freudian school has traditionally fastened on the police as a personification of Chicken Little's superego, I think a Jungian is obliged to see the cry for help as an instinctive plea to the Self. When the ego is in disarray and the persona in tatters, then the inner authority of the Self, in whatever guise deemed necessary, will work toward a balance.[22] As Jung writes:

The psyche does not merely *react*, it gives its own specific answer to the influences at work upon it.[23]

Now, right here is where Adam Brillig's insights are particularly valuable. It was Brillig, you see, who first suggested that Chicken Little's doomsday warning need not be interpreted literally; it could be taken as a symbolic expression of her own inner plight. Which is to say, whether the sky was falling or the earth was rising up, she

---

[20] "A Non-Euclidean Perspective," op. cit., p. 33.

[21] Numerous modern versions have Henny Penny as the heroine, with no mention at all of Chicken Little. These are certainly aberrations—like the frequent misnomer "Chicken Licken"—not supported by a close reading of the stones.

[22] See my *Jung Lexicon: A Primer of Terms and Concepts*, "Self-regulation of the psyche," pp. 120-122..

[23] "Some Crucial Points in Psychoanalysis (A Correspondence between Dr. Jung and Dr. Loÿ)," *Freud and Psychoanalysis*, CW 4, par. 665.

would be caught in the middle. And isn't that, he asks rhetorically, a fitting image of conflict? Stage "two" in the ever-intriguing Axiom of Maria?—

> One becomes two, two becomes three, and out of the third comes the One as the fourth.[24]

From there, according to Brillig, it is but a short step to Jung's theory of neurosis, his views on psychic energy, and the mysterious *tertium non datur* or transcendent function. I concur.[25]

> The clamor reached Ducky Lucky, working in his garden. "What's this cackling all about?" he demanded.
> "The sky is falling!" cried Henny Penny. "A piece of it hit Chicken Little on the head!"
> "That's terrible!" squawked Ducky Lucky.
> And together they all three wailed: "Help! Police! The sky is falling!"
> Their alarums were heard by Goosey Lucy and Gosling Gilbert.
> "What's that?" asked Goosey Lucy and Gosling Gilbert.
> "The sky is falling!" cried Ducky Lucky. "A piece of it hit Chicken Little on the head!"
> "That's terrible!" squawked Goosey Lucy and Gosling Gilbert.
> And now all five wailed: "Help! Police! The sky is falling!"

What a tight concoction. Three new characters—all aspects, psychologically, of Chicken Little herself. Ducky Lucky, whatever his sexual proclivities, is easily seen as an instinctual animus, close to the earth; Goosey Lucy is perhaps a symbolic allusion to the flighty feminine; and Gosling Gilbert, well, what else could he be but her neglected inner child, the potential source of creative energy, yet still buried in an avalanche of civilized accretions? And all seeking help. In Jung's words:

> Too much of the animal distorts the civilized [wo]man, too much civilization makes sick animals.[26]

---

[24] See Jung, *Psychology and Alchemy,* CW 12, par. 209. My own interpretation of this alchemical dictum is presented in *Getting To Know You: The Inside Out of Relationship,* pp. 86-87.

[25] See my outline in *The Survival Papers: Anatomy of a Midlife Crisis,* pp. 11-29, and *Jung Lexicon,* pp. 133-136.

[26] "The Eros Theory," *Two Essays,* CW 7, par. 32.

—giving further credence, I think, to Brillig's seminal notes on Chicken Little as a dissociated neurotic.

> Just then Turkey Lurkey appeared, strutting, stroking his handsome comb.
>
> "You sillies," he said, "you winged stick-heads, feathered furies, stop your fussing and squawking and wailing. If anyone is to call for help, I shall."
>
> And with that he stalked off to the village.

And there the tablets end.

Were the police fetched? We don't know. Did the sky fall? Apparently not—though there is chronological evidence to consider analogies with the Biblical Flood.[27]

Let Chickle Schtick fill in the gaps. For already, you see, we have all we need to support the orthodox Jungian view that the end of the world is an archetypal motif; that is, it may be constellated by circumstances (inner or outer) in anyone or in any culture, at any time and in any place.

As it happens, this was synchronistically confirmed by two personal incidents while I was preparing this paper.

First, my dentist confided to me that mankind was done for.

"Decay," he said, changing drills. "I see it everywhere. We're all going down the tubes."

And then, the very next day, I spoke to my broker.

"Your stocks are down because the Dow Jones is down because the whole world is," she said. "I'm down too. God knows where it will end."

Chicken Little and others have been predicting a falling sky for, what, 7,000 years, and it's still there.

That says something.

---

[27] See A. Heidel, *Chicken Little and Old Testament Parallels,* pp. 78-132.

BOOK ONE

Into the Fire

Alchemical image of the transformation of Mercurius,
as *prima materia,* in the heated, sealed vessel
(Barchusen, *Elementa chemiae,* 1718; National Library, Paris)

"Instead of arguing with the drives which carry us away, we prefer to
cook them and ask them what they want. That can be discovered by
active imagination, or through a fantasy, or through experimenting
in reality, but always with the introverted attitude of observing."

—Marie-Louise von Franz, *Alchemy: An Introduction.*

1
The Letter

I got back from the bank just as Rachel was pulling out. She rolled down her window.

"Sunny hasn't had her walk," she called. "Oh, and there's a special delivery letter on your desk. Don't know who it's from, I didn't open it. Gotta fly!"

And she blew me a kiss, off to her class.

I waved and went in, instantly pleasured by familiar surroundings: old sunglasses lined up on the radiator, elephant prints in the hall; the scuffed mat and stack of slippers; antique chandelier, cut glass doorknobs throwing rainbows; a view from the front door straight through to the back garden.

I've lived here ten years and I'd only been gone half an hour, but was I glad to be back.

Sunny pranced to meet me. She's quite a large dog, about eight years old. She looks like a wolf; she may be a cross between a Collie and a German Shepherd. We don't know anything about her for sure. Rachel picked her out at the pound last year. Sunny barks a lot when people come to the door, but she only bites strange workmen in the garden, when they bend over.

I hung my coat up and went upstairs, mentally greeting the soldier elephants in the window box.

My office was flooded with the afternoon light. A glance told me everything was in order. I checked the fax, turned off the answering machine and picked up the special delivery letter.

The handwriting on the envelope was unfamiliar. There was no sender's name or return address. The few pen strokes had been applied with a flourish, slanting upward from left to right. An optimist, I thought, or perhaps just somewhat inflated. On the back flap were the initials A.B.

I weighed the envelope (it was light) and felt a curious sense of excitement. I became somewhat heady, as if I were stoned.

Well now, I thought, what's this? It's almost twenty years since I had a joint. The feeling grew until I was gripped by such a powerful presentiment that I had to sit down.

"My life is about to change," I thought.

The idea was immediately disturbing, for I am, as may by now be clear, a creature of habit. My life is carefully arranged to keep interruptions at a minimum. My energy is thoughtfully parceled out. Anything new is filtered through Rachel—well, if she's around—who prepares me, if necessary, for the worst.

All in all, I felt distinctly apprehensive.

And yet, at the same time, from deep within there welled up the admission that my life had become all too stagnant. I was comfortable, yes, and quite satisfied with what I had, but perhaps I was going to seed. An adventure might be just the ticket.

Thus, when at last I opened the envelope, I could not at first be sure whether its contents affected me like a breath of fresh air or a disagreeable draft.

It contained a single sheet of paper. The same fluent hand that graced the envelope had written as follows:

> Sir:
>
> I have read your paper on Chicken Little. Bravo! Until now I had believed myself the only person who believed in the existence of more tablets. Now there are two of us! Tomorrow perhaps ten! I know their location and have a plan.
>
> Let me not mince words. We have more than a little in common and there is much work to be done. We must meet! Please contact me as soon as possible.
>
> Adam Brillig, D.Sc., Dipl. Analyt. Psych., Dipl. C.S.[28]

There followed an address and several phone numbers, together with an elaborate timetable indicating where he might be reached during any given day for the next three weeks. At the very bottom there were neat block letters: MS. LITTLE LIVES.

It is difficult to give an accurate description of the effect this had on me.

In the first place, I had thought Adam Brillig was dead. I knew he had received his Diploma in 1956. It was a matter of record that he

---

[28] Diploma in Chickle Schtick.

had established a practice in Boise, Idaho (the first and last Jungian, I believe, to do so). By the time I arrived in Zürich, in the fall of 1974, his reputation as a conservative was well established.[29] No one I knew had seen him at conferences, but I had read his articles in various journals, both Jungian and those devoted to Chickle Schtick. To my knowledge, nothing written by him in either field had been published since his landmark "Non-Euclidean Perspective" on the estimable Ms. Little in 1968.

That was now twenty-four years ago, and since I left Zürich in 1978 his name had not appeared in the International Directory of Jungian Analysts.

Where had Brillig been? Was he still practicing? How old could he be? These questions whirled in my head.

As well, and to be perfectly honest, I had almost forgotten the paper of mine to which Brillig alluded. It was already two years since I wrote it and over a year since it had been published. It was my very first contribution to the world of Chicken Little scholarship. I believe it sprang from a feeling that someone should try to bridge the lamentable gap between Chickle Schtick and Jungian psychology— and the grandiose idea that I was just the one to do it. I was full of it at the time and had eagerly looked forward to whatever response might come. None did.

Now, although flattered by this belated but dramatic show of interest by someone whose work I had the highest regard for, I was more than a little uneasy that my, yes, let me admit it, somewhat whimsical piece, which had already faded in my memory, should be taken so seriously.

I dug my paper out and read it through, nodding to myself. I had to smile at the bits attributed to "Janet Marble" and "A.G. Grandize." As I recall, they were Rachel's doing.

---

[29] There are different interpretations of what a "conservative" Jungian is. Personally, I understand it to mean someone who adheres closely to Jung's expressed views. I have no reason to doubt that Brillig felt the same. When he was criticized by Kleinians, Kohutians and so-called post-Jungians for being "too doctrinaire" (i.e., not open to new ideas), he replied: "I see no need to reinvent the wheel. It isn't that Jung was never wrong, rather he was always right." [*American Journal of Analytical Psychology,* vol. 13, no. 4 (Fall 1965), p. 145]

"It has something," she'd mused, reading my initial draft, "but it could use some spice." And she made a few suggestions.

I was reluctant at first. Whimsy is one thing, but playing with the truth is something else. On the other hand, Rachel is, to some extent, "She-who-must-be-obeyed."[30] In the end I met her half way, which is to say I took her advice.

Now I focused on the passage that had apparently prompted Brillig to write:

> . . . stone tablets discovered in Lower Kraznac. . . . Some tablets are whole, others are merely fragments. There are huge gaps. The first seems to start in mid-story, and the seventh ends so abruptly that one cannot help but think that others are still to be found.

God, I thought, where did that come from—"others are still to be found"? I wracked my brain and came up empty. It was a throwaway line, surely, just to show I knew my Chickle Schtick.

Now here was the expert, calling my bluff.

I was not happy.

I got Sunny's leash, stuffed a plastic bag in my pocket—being a conscientious stoop and scooper—and took her out to the park.

Arnold came at my call. He kicked off his galoshes and threw his coat on a chair. I showed him Brillig's letter. He borrowed my glasses and read it through without comment, then gave me a great clap on the arm.

"Don't panic," he said. "Let's have a drink."

Arnold's a bear of a man. We're more than close. We shared a house in Zürich when we were training. Now we practice together as colleagues. He sees things in ways I don't, and vice versa. He designed my garden and taught me to appreciate free verse. I showed him how to sew and make cookies, read maps, fix lamps. He taught

---

[30] This is a phrase Jung lifted from the writer Rider Haggard to describe the authority of a man's anima, his inner woman. (See, for instance, *Two Essays on Analytical Psychology,* par. 189.) I was amused to see it echoed recently in the popular PBS television series, "Rumpole of the Bailey," where Rumpole's wife, entirely innocuous to the viewer, is routinely referred to by him as "She-who-must-be-obeyed." I use it here, of course, somewhat tongue in cheek. Rachel is flesh and blood, my anima isn't. I know the difference, only at times, like Rumpole, I'm liable to forget.

me that being late, or not showing up at all, wasn't a criminal offense. I instructed him in how to make cinnamon toast and boil an egg.[31]

Arnold and I have had our disagreements, for sure, but being with him puts me in touch with sides of myself that are otherwise a closed book. Projection, I suppose some would call it. The power to constellate, says Arnold.

Come to think of it, he had had a significant hand in my Chicken Little paper.

"Well," said Arnold, crashing on the sofa with that boyish grin he has. "Looks like you're on the line, old boy."

"It would help if you said we," I replied.

Rachel came back about six. She found us face to face in the living room, going at it. Arnold was on his third tumbler of straight Scotch choked with ice. I was sipping mint tea to keep my head clear. There were papers everywhere, notes on this and that. A good half of Jung's *Collected Works* were on the floor, sharing space with von Franz, books on mythology, cheese and cracker crumbs and writings on Chicken Little.

I greeted Rachel and rolled my eyes.

All afternoon Arnold had been pushing possibilities. I had listened intently, taking careful notes, as usual, while resisting, as usual. Okay, so he's intuitive and I'm not, but I've been bewitched by Arnold more than once and I'm gun-shy. He'd been suggesting things that would certainly disturb my life and what's more might ruin my reputation.

Now he threw up his hands.

"So it's not entirely safe. But don't you see? That's exactly what you need!"

"Thou sayest!" I shot back.

That's one of Arnold's favorite rejoinders, meaning, "That's the way *you* see it, with *your* complexes, *your* typology, *your* background," and so on. I sometimes use it just to make him mad.

"I have quite enough on my plate, thank you," I said.

---

[31] These few lines do scant justice to the author's long-standing association with Arnold, which is a recurring theme in my *Survival Papers* and *Dear Gladys: The Survival Papers, Book 2.*

I followed Rachel into the kitchen, where she was pouring herself a spritzer. I dished some food into Sunny's bowl and told Rachel about Brillig's letter. She shook her auburn hair and smiled.

"I wouldn't dismiss it out of hand," she said.

I have a lot of respect for Rachel. She has a graduate degree in Fine Arts and is quick witted. She's ten years younger than me. On tip-toes she barely reaches my chin. She's developing into quite a good painter. After only two years on the market she's already self-supporting. We met at a mutual friend's party, the year after I returned from Zürich. We danced together and that was it.

Rachel and I have been through a lot. We're not married and we don't live together, but we've had six children, all now out on their own. Thinking isn't her superior function, but it's not bad. Her intuition is pretty good and I trust her feeling. We have a workable relationship. She's interested in what I do, and vice versa. She's rather more extraverted than I am, but we share an earthy appreciation for life. And we're friends.

We hugged and Rachel went to freshen up.

Arnold joined me in the kitchen and opened a bottle of the wine he'd brought, *Canepa,* a cabernet sauvignon from Chile. We talked about baseball while I put a meal together. Arnold's a fervent fan of the Toronto Blue Jays. He told me the Jays had just won the World Series, of all things, and wasn't that fantastic?

I pounded the wall and jumped up and down. I didn't really care one way or the other—I prefer cribbage or scrabble—but Arnold's excitement is infectious.

Over dinner Rachel told us about the new print-making class she was teaching. Arnold plied her with questions. Rachel drew sketches on napkins to describe various techniques. I listened and made a comment or two, but on the whole my mind was elsewhere; it kept reverting to Adam Brillig.

Rachel cleared the table and made a pot of tea. I put on a Bach flute concerto and rolled a cigarette. Arnold nursed a Drambuie. Sunny prowled the room, hunting for scraps.

"I was just wondering," I said, "if Frau B. was at the Institute when Brillig was there."

Arnold hooted.

Frau B. was the Administrative Secretary, an officious woman in her late sixties. We called her Baba Yaga. She scolded you for whatever you did or didn't do. She would not bend the rules; she insisted on following rigorous procedures to the letter, and when you finally thought you had everything in order she'd find some obscure regulation to prove you'd forgotten to dot an i or cross a t. She treated everyone as naughty children. If you could stand up to her, it was said, you could get through the training.

The male trainees had an especially hard time with Baba Yaga. It took all our courage to approach her, cap in hand, about anything. Doctors of divinity, English professors, middle-aged physicians, we all left her office cursing and sweating. You knew you'd get a tongue-lashing at first, but if you were very lucky you might leave with a pat on the head.

"Do you remember what happened when I first went to register?" said Arnold. "She told me my name wasn't on the list, I'd have to go back to Canada and reapply?"

"Yes, you spotted your application filed under your Christian name—but then you couldn't find the Swiss visa granting you student status and your receipt for lecture fees."

"She closed my file and turned away," said Arnold. " *'Es tut mir leid,'* she said, patting her coif. 'I'm sorry, you're just not ready. I'm very busy, *danke,* thank you very much. Come back when you have yourself in order.' "

Arnold fumed. Baba Yaga pushed him out and locked the door in his face. He found his visa and receipt in his shaving kit and went back the next day.

"Herr Arnold?" She squinted from him to her list. *"Nichts.* Nobody by that name."

Arnold stabbed the desk. "That's me," he growled, "and if you don't like it you can piss up your sleeve."

Baba Yaga smiled and stamped his application.

"You're a nice boy," she said. *"Viele glück."*

I learned a lot about myself from having to deal with Frau B. My analyst helped, he gave me the right perspective. He was on the Curatorium, the governing body of the Institute.

"That woman is mad!" I raged. "Why don't you get rid of her?"

"It's not her," he said, "it's her animus. You must learn to tell the difference. She herself has a kind heart. Her animus does not." And he read to me from Jung:

> No matter how friendly and obliging a woman's Eros may be, no logic on earth can shake her if she is ridden by the animus. Often the man has the feeling—and he is not altogether wrong—that only seduction or a beating or rape would have the necessary power of persuasion.[32]

"Think of her—or him, if you like," said my analyst, "as the dragon that guards the treasure. A sharp tongue is like a dragon breathing fire. It's the hero's task to outwit the dragon. Frau B. is in the right place, she separates the men from the boys."

Indeed, and in the end I even came to like her.

Arnold and I like recalling the old days. It reminds us of where we've been.

Meanwhile, Rachel had been rooting around in the mess on the floor. Now she came up with one of Brillig's early papers and motioned us to be quiet.

"Listen to this," she said.

> It is common knowledge that the Grail is not only the fabled "lost" container of Christ's blood, but also a powerful symbol for the highest aspirations of Western man. Though I am not a Christian and have little time for the arguably spurious revelations of the Gospels, I accept their metaphoric weight. Unfortunately, nothing of the sort has been historically accorded to Ms. Little. On the contrary, she and her poignant tale have been virtually ignored. Is this evidence of a sexist bias? Racist? Chicken phobia? Even, perhaps, a patriarchal plot?
>
> I urge Chickle Schtickers to pursue these inquiries with vigor. We have nowhere to go but up.[33]

Arnold laughed and helped himself to a an inch of schnapps.

---

[32] "The Syzygy: Anima and Animus," *Aion*, CW 9ii, par. 29. I've never really cared much for that interpolation ("and he is not altogether wrong"). Still, I think Jung accurately captured a man's primitive reaction to an abrasive woman.

[33] "Innocent Icon: C. Little and the Holy Grail," *International Journal of Chickle Schtick,* vol. 12, no. 2 (Spring 1958), p. 108.

"Brillig must be over eighty by now," he said.

"Here's another," said Rachel, and read:

Nothing so beguiles the mind as the manner in which Chicken Little came into the world, except perhaps the enigmatic way in which she left it. She comes from nowhere and goes nowhere. That is the beauty of Ms. Little.[34]

"Sounds like he was heavily invested in this stuff," said Rachel.

"From his letter," said Arnold, "he still is."

I nodded.

"Where Chicken Little is concerned, it would seem that Brillig is what we'd call complexed," I said. "A cognitive psychologist might say his reactions are 'over-determined,' but it comes to the same thing: he can't leave it—or her—alone."

"Obsessive-compulsive, perhaps?" suggested Arnold.

"Call it what you want, I've been there—utterly consumed by thoughts of Chicken Little. Before that, when I was ten, it was my stamp collection, then Captain Marvel, then science fiction, then girls, then Kafka, then Jung, then elephants, then Rachel, then . . ."

"What's lu-min-ous, is nu-min-ous," sang Arnold. He had found a bottle of Cointreau I'd been saving for my father's birthday. He poured himself a healthy shot.

"The point is," I said, "we all have complexes. There's nothing wrong with that."[35]

"I don't think that's in dispute," said Rachel, looking at Arnold.

Arnold yawned.

"The question is," said Rachel, "will we cooperate with Brillig—collude, encourage, whatever . . . ?"

She looked at me. "Well?"

Silence fell on our party of three.

I don't know what was going on in them, but personally I was of two minds.

---

[34] "The Kraznac Tablets in Light of the Dead Sea Scrolls," *Harvest Historical Review,* vol. 14, no. 3 (Summer 1960), p. 38.

[35] I trust this bald dinner-table remark among friends, to make a particular point, will not be held against me. In fact, complexes are probably the root of all evil. See Jung, "A Review of the Complex Theory," *The Structure and Dynamics of the Psyche,* CW 8, or my *Jung Lexicon,* pp. 37-39.

I am not adventurous. I hew to known ground. I haven't camped
since the morning in Brittany when I was faced at daybreak by a
cow. I don't like hiking. My life was already full. I had the publishing business, a small practice and a few close friends, a garden to
work in and a summer retreat. The books took a lot of time, but I
could usually manage a few hours off to play snooker.

Though Arnold might characterize my life as "a bit tight"—as that
very afternoon he had—I liked to think of it as nicely contained. To
me, Brillig's proposition spelled chaos. What if he wanted to haul
me off to Carpathia? I didn't even know where it was.

Nevertheless, the feeling that overtook me before opening his letter was still around: Maybe I did need a change. In my mind's ear I
heard Jung saying what I myself have quoted to others more than
once: "The good is always the enemy of the better. . . . If better is to
come, good must stand aside."[36]

Rachel spoke first.

"He's an old man. Don't we at least owe him the courtesy to hear
what he has to say?"

I looked at Arnold.

"You know where I stand," he said, fumbling for his shoes.
"Say, could I trouble one of you to drive me home?"

I didn't phone Brillig because I wanted more time to chew on it.
Rachel and Arnold were clearly interested, but I was still ambivalent.
True, I respected what I knew of Brillig's scholarship, but what if he
was nuts? Being an analyst is a guarantee of nothing. Like Chicken
Little, Jung attracts a lot of wierdoes. Brillig had a Diploma, so
what? I have reservations about many of my colleagues. Arnold goes
further: "They're all crazy except you and me. And I'm not sure
about you."

On the other hand, even if Brillig was quite sane, why would I put
my energy into something so . . . so open-ended? I'm a distinctly
linear man. Going from A to B in a straight line is just my cup of tea.
Oh, I wouldn't deny the value to others of meandering, the goalless
pleasure of the byways, going with the flow and so on. Good luck to

---

[36] "The Development of Personality," *The Development of Personality,* CW
17, par. 320.

them, I say. But that's not me. I'm at home on the beaten track.

Besides, my interest in Chickle Schtick was, after all, at a low point. My current studies in that area were desultory, at best. And I had more than enough to do without going off on a wild, well, chicken chase.

The whole business kept me awake for days.[37] I'm afraid even Rachel became impatient.

"You're a grown man," she grumbled, as once again I crawled over her in the middle of the night and got dressed to go home. "Make up your mind."

Arnold was marginally more sympathetic.

"Here's what Jung says," and he read out loud:

> The stirring up of conflict is a Luciferian virtue in the true sense of the word. Conflict engenders fire, the fire of affects and emotions, and like every other fire it has two aspects, that of combustion and that of creating light.[38]

"You see?" said Arnold. "It's good for you."

I finally wrote to Brillig, as follows.

Dear Sir,

Let me say first of all that I felt honored to hear from you. I still remember your remarkable thesis, "Archetypal Motifs in Existentialism," which I had the opportunity to read in the Institute library. It is an impressive study, which I often heard students quote passages from in colloquia. You will not be surprised, I'm sure, to learn that the profs were not always pleased! In fact, I once stood up for you myself in a discussion of Jung's philosophical antecedents. (I was slapped down unmercifully, to my mind, but that's another story.)

I have to tell you, too, that your letter took me completely by surprise. My little piece on "Ms. Little," as you so charmingly refer to her, was written at a time when I naively believed I knew something about the subject. My studies in that area have since lapsed and

---

[37] For the record, this has happened to me before. The last time, I forfeited a $500 deposit on a new car. The salesman was quite perturbed when I told him I couldn't go through with it. "Makes no sense to me," he said, "it's a fine machine." "I don't doubt that," I blushed, "but my dreams do."

[38] "Psychological Aspects of the Mother Archetype," *The Archetypes and the Collective Unconscious,* CW 9i, par. 179.

I had almost forgotten it.

I must also confess an embarrassing truth: I have no idea whence came my seemingly confident observation that other tablets "are still to be found." My original notes have long since disappeared, I'm afraid. My colleague Arnold, who assisted me in the research, believes it was an intuitive leap. I frankly doubt this, since I am predominantly a sensation type. Personally, I think Arnold slipped it in when I wasn't looking, though he denies this. (What can you do, he's a friend.)

Finally, I have to tell you that I am averse to travel. I get homesick going to the corner store. I do not like climbing mountains and avoid reading about them; even small hills make me nauseous. Years of analysis have not stilled my terror of heights. The thought of trekking bores me.

I also have a pretty full agenda these days, what with my practice and the books (catalogue enclosed).

The bottom line here, though I might wish it otherwise, is that I don't see how I can be of any help to you.

I sent this off with a heavy heart. That told me I wasn't sure I'd made the right decision. I should have stewed more, held the tension longer, waited for Jung's "transcendent function"—a solution from within, not from the head.

"Never mind," soothed Rachel, "you tried."

2
The Meeting

It was a slow week. Arnold came by a couple of times to shoot the breeze or talk about his dreams. I ask his advice on mine too. Being so unalike, we can often spot each other's blind spots.

Rachel was busy with her classes. Business was slow to sluggish. I cleaned up the mailing list and culled the files. I raked the leaves and canned beets. I made long lists of things to do when I felt like it. I walked Sunny and watched old movies on television.

I kept my own counsel and slept a lot.

Brillig's fax, late on a Monday afternoon, woke me up. My apprehension grew as it rolled slowly out.

Dear Friend (if I may be so bold),
    My heart leaped at your reply. Nothing could have made me happier! I shall be arriving late Friday afternoon. I would be obliged if you would arrange accommodation. I implore you to free yourself for the weekend.

Adam Brillig, D.Sc., Dipl. Analyt. Psych., Dipl. C.S.

P.S. I shall be with my assistant. He's green but shows potential.

I could write here, in pulp-fiction fashion, something like, "My heart fell," or "I was dumb-struck," but nothing close to adequate comes to mind.

Rachel found me in twilight.
"He's coming anyway," I said, showing her the fax.
She read it and giggled.
"Put them in the attic with the squirrels."
I grimaced, but in truth I was grateful to Rachel for trying to lighten my mood. What she didn't know was that I had been scared to death that Brillig wouldn't take the hint, that he might follow up with something else to keep me awake.
I called Arnold to give him the news. He laughed.
"What are you worried about?" he said. "You could fax him back

and tell him to go fly a kite."

Well, strictly speaking, I could.

But to tell the truth, by then I had realized that in spite of every-thing, *some part of me deep down firmly believed in the existence of more tablets;* and indeed, that part of me was considerably more ex-cited than scared.

Both Rachel and Arnold were invaluable in the next few days. Rachel offered to put together a file of Brillig's articles on Chicken Little; Arnold said he'd help. It was left to me to cross-reference these with Jung's *Collected Works* and to assemble what was public knowledge about Professor Adam Brillig.[39] We worked at all this late into the night.

On Thursday evening I asked, "And where will they stay?"

I eyed Rachel, who had just done up her basement. Arnold lived in one large room.

Rachel said it made her nervous to have strangers under her roof. I suggested she might make an effort for my sake. And why should she? she said—I had loads of space.

I reminded her of my near-pathological need for privacy and that house-guests were anathema to me. So book them into a hotel, said Rachel. I said that would be insulting. Rachel said if they felt in-sulted that was their problem. I said well, maybe *they* wouldn't feel insulted, but I'd feel bad. Rachel said maybe I had a problem in that area—being liked. I said I had no problem at all in being liked, it was more a question of what was politically correct. Rachel said that was really a laugh.

Arnold said, In for a penny, in for a pound, and looked at the ceiling.

It was finally decided they would stay on my third floor. I put clean sheets on the beds, vacuumed, made the walls respectable and turned the heat on.

---

[39] With limited time, my major sources were, obviously, *Who's Who in Chickle Schtick, 1940-1990,* and proceedings of Jungian conferences. I turned up very little I didn't already know. Brillig seemed to have dropped out of sight about 1970. Only after considerable time with him was I able to flesh out the early gaps and later years. Interested readers will find a com-prehensive dossier in *The Compleat Brillig* (in preparation).

Everything was in place by 5 p.m. Friday. The fireplace was laid and the dining room table was set; Rachel had adorned it with imported lilies and daffodils. Five candlesticks were ready in their Mexican brass holders.

My prime rib, glazed with mustard and honey and heavily laced with garlic, was on low heat, dripping its juice onto roast potatoes, button onions and carrots. Rachel had prepared a plate of mixed cheese and biscuits, with olives, sweet radish and dill pickles on the side, garnished with parsley. Arnold was due any minute.

I lit the fire. Rachel talked about the meeting with her agent, at which they had worked out details for her next show. I told her where I was in my book, well, as much as I thought I could risk; it was still pretty fragile.

Sunny lay at our feet with ears perked, looking from one to the other. Rachel says that when Sunny's not asleep or eating, she's studying for her Ph.D. in us.

Rachel worked on a sketch. I finished off a crossword puzzle and then fidgeted.

"Supposed to snow tonight," said Rachel.

"Early for snow," I said.

"That's what the papers say too."

"Do you suppose there's time for some Scrabble?" I asked.

We both jumped at the knock. Sunny barked up a storm. Rachel collared and soothed her. I opened the door. A taxi was pulling out of the driveway.

Two men in dark cloaks stood on the porch. One limped forward: slight build, little taller than a dwarf; elderly, thick salt and pepper goatee, almost entirely bald. Definitely gnomish. He looked up at me with a calm, penetrating gaze and vigorously grasped my hand.

"Adam Brillig," he bowed slightly, proffering a large bouquet of iris, then turned, "and this is my assistant, Norman."

A tall, lean man with dark hair, mid-forties, stepped into the light. I recognized the face immediately. Norman! My goodness, what a surprise. He'd been in analysis with me a few years back.[40] We'd lost touch when he went off to study in Zürich. He greeted me warmly, with a firm grip.

---

[40] Our time together is the subject of my *Survival Papers* and *Dear Gladys.*

"Rachel," I said, "you remember Norman?"

"I sure do," said Rachel, smiling.

She took the flowers to the kitchen and I helped Norman carry several large suitcases into the hall. Sunny scampered from pillar to post, sniffing.

At that moment Arnold arrived. More introductions. I took coats and hung them in the closet. Norman was wearing a black turtleneck, Brillig a tartan waistcoat, white shirt and mauve bow tie. Arnold had on a track suit, he'd just come from the gym. Rachel and I weren't dressed that casually.

I ushered them into the living room, where the warm fire dispelled the late autumn chill.

Brillig was immediately struck by Rachel's paintings and my elephant collection. Rachel pointed out two of my prize pieces, the one I'd found on a rainy day in Zürich, on my way to James Joyce's grave, and a 300-year old solid ivory bull given to me by my very first analysand. Norman noted that I had a few new ones since he'd been here, then engaged Arnold in a discussion of Pethick originals, of which my house sports several.[41]

I took requests for drinks and left Rachel to do the guided tour.

It was a lively evening, not to say boisterous. Arnold had brought several bottles of French burgundy. Brillig recognized the cellar and regaled us with tales of gastronomic delights in Dijon and his experience motoring along the *Route des Grands Crus,* which he said passes through many of the finest vineyards in the world.

Appetites were robust; my simple meal was lauded.

"The food, the flowers, the setting!" enthused Brillig. He stood up and proposed a toast.

"I thank you"—his nod including Rachel, Arnold and I—"and feel honored."

Norman seconded that. We drained our glasses and Arnold went around the table with refills.

---

[41] J. Pethick is a Canadian artist known for his inventive three-dimensional illusionary devices. Examples of his work may be seen on the covers of my *Dear Gladys;* Joseph Henderson, *Cultural Attitudes in Psychological Perspective;* James Hollis, *The Middle Passage: From Misery to Meaning in Midlife;* and Carole Chambers, *Still Life Under the Occupation.*

The conversation ranged from painting to psychology to ethnology, interspersed with philosophical reflections, snippets of arcane Chickle Schtick and travel anecdotes. Brillig had spent some time in his youth roaming the lower slopes of the world's great mountains. Rachel had toured Tibet for several weeks the year before. Brillig said he knew it well. Norman and Arnold discovered with glee that both had ancestors who'd lived in Wales.

Flushed with meat, fine drink and good company, I relaxed. My apprehension vanished.

The nature of the relationship between Norman and Brillig was not immediately clear, though they were obviously close in spite of the difference in age. At first I kept getting flashbacks of Norman as I used to know him, but these were soon blotted out by how well he carried himself. It turned out that he had stayed in Zürich for only a few months.

"The lectures weren't to my taste," he said, somewhat apologetically, "and I felt lost without German. But"—and here his eyes lit up—"I was very taken with the Niederdorf."[42]

He had returned and gone back to school to study photography. For the past few years he had made a good living working freelance. I gathered he had met Brillig while on assignment for the National Geographic.

On the whole, Norman held his own on practical issues, but otherwise was deferential to Brillig. I didn't wonder why. Adam Brillig took my breath away. It was clearly his evening.

There was evident in Brillig's manner of thinking, as in his outward appearance, a singular combination of self-contained maturity and the openness of a child. His mind was a force as palpable as heat or light or wind. This was manifested in an exceptional faculty for seeing ideas as external objects—and vice versa—and for establishing striking connections between concepts which to me appeared totally unrelated. One moment he treated human history as a logical progression akin to a problem in quantum mechanics; in the next breath he expounded on the method of divination using chicken entrails, and convincingly linked this with the essentially religious search for meaning.

---

[42] The "lower town" area in the center of Zürich, known for its night life.

"May I?" he asked, moving toward my bookshelf. He pulled out Jung's *Psychology and Religion* and leafed through it. "Ah, here we are," and he read:

> We might say . . . that the term "religion" designates the attitude peculiar to a consciousness which has been changed by experience of the *numinosum.* [43]

"Well now, we know all about that, don't we?" he said.
I threw a finger at Arnold; he threw it right back.

At one point Brillig jumped up and motioned to Norman. Together they pulled their largest case—virtually a trunk—into the living room. Brillig opened it and unceremoniously dumped its contents on the floor.

There emerged a most disparate collection of objects, constituting a veritable encyclopedia of what passes for human knowledge: cards or diagrams of plant cells, Mendeleev's periodic table of elements, a key-code to Chinese brush-strokes, the cross-section of a snail, Lorentz's transformation formulae; sheets of Mayan hieroglyphics, economic and demographic statistics, musical scores, the ground plan of the Great Pyramid; phonetic charts, genealogies, road maps of major cities; small fossil remains, plant specimens in amber, delicate watercolors of termites, axolotls, rare marsupials; several pocket dictionaries, illustrated guides to Chartres Cathedral and the Vatican, a Tarot deck, yarrow stalks for the I Ching, star charts, labeled knots of rope; paint brushes and miniature palettes, a joke book, postcards of fine art.

Everything, in short, bespeaking the mental agility of a twentieth-century Leonardo.

Brillig eyed the pile with satisfaction.

"I don't travel light," he said.

The cornucopian display made me quite giddy. Rachel gave a delighted cry and settled down for a closer look.

---

[43] "Psychology and Religion," CW 11, par. 9. The Latin *numinosum* refers to a dynamic agency or effect independent of the conscious will. Its English derivatives are "numinous" and "numinosity." Needless to say, every complex carries with it a degree of numinosity; otherwise it wouldn't be a complex, it would be something else. Exactly *what* else it might be is the subject of considerable disagreement, even among Jungians.

"Mind you," said Brillig with a sardonic smile, "it's all fake. One can't say with any certainty of any item here that it contains the 'truth.' In the whole lot there is nothing but mystery and error. Where one ends, the other begins."

Returning to the table and helping himself to more roast beef (he chose only the rarest bits), Brillig confessed he had great difficulty with intuitions not backed by concrete reality. I was attentive because I'm in the same boat myself.

Norman coughed.

"I call it the Brillig Principle: 'Whatever is not supported by experience is not true.' "

"That is my belief," said Brillig, "hence I am sometimes overwhelmed by what *might* happen."

He emphasized *might,* he said, because he didn't trust his premonitions, even though some had subsequently proven to be true.

I got quite excited.

"But that's just the way people reacted to Chicken Little!"

"Yes," nodded Brillig, stroking his goatee. "Ironic, isn't it?"

Then he leaned toward me so we were cheek and jowl.

"Ms. Little, you know," he whispered, "personifies the repressed side of God."

Rachel, still on the floor, overheard and gasped.

Arnold stopped chewing and looked up. "What was that?"

Brillig waved his hand.

"A heavy subject. Let us leave it for another time. We have grave decisions to make, decisions which I believe will have far-reaching consequences for all our lives. First we must get to know each other. Later, *Deo concedente,* we shall have the opportunity to act and suffer together. This evening it is enough to make one's acquaintance, as they say."

Over a freshly-ground mix of Columbian coffee and Arabian decaf, served with real whipped cream on Rachel's apple crumble, I put Brillig on the spot.

"Professor Brillig, I looked you up. I could find nothing by or about you since 1970. Have you retired, then?"

"Please, Adam will do. Retired? Norman, did you hear that? Oh my goodness no! I do contract work in various factories, a mountain-climbing goods store, a chemical laboratory, a photo-engraving shop. In each place I undertake the apparently impossible. I'm paid badly, of course, I'm too old to bargain, but I own the patents to whatever I invent. I must keep active, you see; it's one way to know who I am."

"When I was about six," I said, "I fell asleep in the bathroom and dreamed I woke up dead, wondering who I'd been."

"A case in point," said Brillig.

He went over to the pile on the floor and pulled out a book that had obviously been well-thumbed.

"This is *Mount Analogue,* by the French writer René Daumal, whose untimely demise in 1944—gracious, he was only thirty-six, my own age at the time—was a tragic loss to literature."

Brillig read:

> I can admit to you that I fear death. Not what we *imagine* about death, for such fear is itself imaginary. And not my death as it will be set down with a date in the public records. But that death I suffer every moment, the death of that voice which, out of the depths of my childhood, keeps questioning me as it does you: "Who am I" Everything in and around us seems to conspire to strangle it once and for all. Whenever that voice is silent—and it doesn't speak often— I'm an empty body, a perambulating carcass. I'm afraid that one day it will fall silent, or that it will speak too late.[44]

"We all wonder in the early years," said Brillig, "but you know how it is; as we grow older we lose touch with the inner life. Overwhelmed by practical matters and the opinions of others, we forget the mystery. Just as in your dream, we might, any of us, wake up to find ourselves dead."

He gently closed the book and lowered his eyes.

Rachel was quite moved. So was I.

"Do you still do analysis?" asked Arnold.

"No one since—." Brillig nodded at Norman. "Not my greatest success, I'm afraid." He laughed uproariously. "Ah well, I think we get along."

Norman smiled. I gathered this was a private joke.

---

[44] *Mount Analogue,* p. 35.

"But why did you stop?" pressed Arnold.

"My dear fellow, there is a time for everything. I was not born to be a sounding-board for others. I was not a psychologist by training or inclination. I became an analyst purely by chance, or so it seemed at the time. As we know, there is very little in one's life that happens fortuitously."

"Would it be presumptuous," said Arnold, uncorking yet another *Auberge de Jeunesse* (1982), "to ask if you went to Zürich on your knees?"

"Dear sir! Indeed I did. I went there to save myself. When I left, re-membered, as it were, I was somewhat better equipped than before to weather what Shakespeare euphemistically called the 'slings and arrows of outrageous fortune.' I was certainly not whole, of course, but who is?"

The old adage came to mind and I threw it out.

"In the land of the blind, the one-eyed man is king."

"Quite so," nodded Brillig.

He accepted Rachel's offer of another helping of crumble.

"I practiced for many years. To those who came, I gave my best. Executives, housewives, taxi-drivers, teachers, actors, politicians—truly a cross-section of the human soul. I believe they got their money's worth. You understand I was not interested in people en masse, only in individuals. There were many worthy causes for which others marched in the street—as once I did myself—but I no longer had energy for that. Analytic work was endlessly fascinating—who has ever seen the same dream twice?—but of course I didn't do it only for them, it was important to me too."

He fell silent.

"And then?" prompted Rachel.

"Ah yes, and then," said Brillig.

I must say here that this was one of the things I liked most about this engaging old man. He had no glib answers. He was not afraid to keep silent when there was nothing to say, nor to reflect at length before speaking. In this report of the evening, I would not like to give the impression that he just ran on to a captive audience, as it were; there were long periods when he seemed more than content to listen to someone else.

Arnold furtively slipped his plate to Sunny. Norman toyed with a spoon, eyeing Rachel. Rachel's attention was focused on Brillig, who finally spoke.

"To my mind," he said, "Jung's basic tenet, to which I have always adhered and God help me always will, is"—and he quoted from memory:

> What is it, at this moment and in this individual, that represents the natural urge of life? That is the question [which] neither science, nor worldly wisdom, nor religion, nor the best of advice can resolve.[45]

I knew the passage well. I looked at Arnold, who nodded back. It was our feeling in a nutshell.

"That's just how we feel—in a nutshell," I said.

"So you see," said Brillig, "when I found my mind wandering in analytic sessions, I had to ask myself: What would I rather be doing? Where does my energy really want to go?"

He paused as Arnold refilled his snifter from the flagon of four star Napoleon brandy Brillig had earlier produced, with a flourish, from one of their bags.

"Thank you. As you know, the answer to that question is not discovered overnight. Even a seasoned professional, which by that time I could fairly claim to be, may find it necessary to go back into the fire."

"I reckon," said Arnold, "that even the most thorough analysis is only good for about ten years."

"Oh," I teased, "that's why you've been so cranky lately. You're way overdue."

"As are you, my friend," grinned Arnold.

"You may well be right," Brillig nodded to Arnold. "Something new and unforeseen is always coming up. We have the tools, yes, we certainly have the tools," he sighed, "but we get so caught up in using them in the service of others that we forget to use them for ourselves."

I squirmed, though without letting on, just as I used to when my analyst hit the mark.

---

[45] "The Structure of the Unconscious," *Two Essays on Analytical Psychology,* CW 7, pars. 488-489.

"Naturally I thought of working with a colleague," said Brillig, "but there was no one who commanded my respect. I was obliged to fall back on my own resources. I resumed recording my dreams, which I had woefully neglected. I spent hours reflecting on the images, amplifying them, recording my thoughts and feelings. Well, you know the routine—all those things one does as a matter of course in analysis. I got back into active imagination. I started painting again, playing with clay, carving wood. In short, I became totally self-absorbed."

"No offense," said Rachel, "but I know people who would call that narcissistic."

Brillig smiled.

"My dear, who can deny it? To some extent self-involvement always is. But unconscious narcissism is a far cry from a conscious act of self-preservation. I dare say you will recall Christ's admonition to the poor soul he found working his garden on the Sabbath? 'If you don't know what you are doing, you are damned; if you do, you are blessed.' I knew I was in trouble, you see—deep *schtuck,* as some would say—and when that happens, in my experience the best way to get back on track is to turn the spotlight on yourself."

"I think it's to your credit that you recognized the problem," offered Norman.

"That's as may be," said Brillig. "In any case, I took on no new patients. My practice slowly diminished, by attrition. When I had found my way, I closed the door on that chapter of my life. That was, let me see . . . Norman?"

"Twelve years ago?"

"Yes, so it was. Oh, I've kept my hand in, here and there, now and then. Norman, for instance. We still work together, though not in the usual way."

I looked at Norman. He gave nothing away.

"And your interest in Jung?" asked Arnold.

Brillig shrugged.

"That has not flagged."

"There is much talk these days of going beyond Jung," I said, "of breaking new ground."

"My dear fellow," said Brillig, "There is talk these days of many things, 'of shoes and ships and sealing wax,' as Lewis Carroll said.[46] Depth psychology has become a free-for-all, there is little discrimination. I find it difficult to take seriously the undergraduate gropings of those who don't know Jung. Why break new ground, I ask, when his topsoil has barely been tilled?"

"Perhaps it is a matter of opinion," said Arnold.

"Opinions," said Brillig "are as plentiful as turnips and worth about as much. I have a great respect for facts. These so-called New Agers simply muddy the waters with their crystals and channeling and, oh horror!—vision quests. You understand I have nothing against visions that come unbidden—goodness knows I've had enough of them myself—but I don't see the point in going out looking, like some great Easter egg hunt."

I agreed. "There seem to be groups and workshops for just about everything. Do you know, I recently received a notice about an organization dedicated to the recovery of lost foreskin."

"I remember that," laughed Rachel. "It didn't even mention circumcision."

"The soul is a delicate flower," said Brillig. "It flourishes in solitude, in nature and in intense work, one-on-one, with a mentor; it seldom manifests in groups."

"I do think there is a legitimate desire for change," I said, "for some kind of personal transformation."

"Yes," said Brillig, "I dare say, and I'm sure we all welcome that. Alas, I fear there is a tendency to mistake temporarily heightened awareness for rebirth. As Jung pointed out—and he was certainly not the first—the group experience does not last."[47]

" 'The fates guide the willing,' " chipped in Arnold, quoting one of Seneca's aphorisms, " 'the unwilling they drag.' "[48]

Norman said that reminded him of Jung's observation, that "anyone who is destined to descend into a deep pit had better set about it with all the necessary precautions rather than risk falling into the hole backwards."[49]

---

[46] *Through the Looking Glass, and What Alice Found There,* p. 78.
[47] "Psychology and Religion," *Psychology and Religion,* CW 11, par. 226.
[48] *Epistola,* 107, II.
[49] *Aion,* CW 9ii, par. 125.

To which I added one of my own favorites: "The psychological rule says that when an inner situation is not made conscious, it happens outside, as fate."[50]

After that pot pourri the conversation turned to a discussion of contemporary art. This was Rachel's forum. She held forth at some length on why she did what she did. Then she gave a lively demonstration of how she did it.

I listened and watched and was happy for her.

It was well after midnight when I showed Norman and Brillig to their quarters. My third floor consists of a bathroom flanked by two small rooms. It did used to be an attic, but after a tasteful renovation it's quite cozy.

We paused on the landing.

"I believe the squirrels have decamped," I said. "I'm still working on the mice."

Brillig smiled and held out his hand.

"It has been a most enjoyable evening," he said, with undisguised emotion. "I thank you for putting us up. I am mindful of the inconvenience and trust you will have no cause for regret. Tomorrow we shall get down to brass tacks."

He bowed in that engaging old world manner and closed the door. Norman said he was thankful to have been so warmly received and disappeared into the other room.

In bed I snuggled up to Rachel. She responded and we had our way. Drifting off to sleep, I was full of thoughts.

"Thanks for all your help tonight," I murmured.

"It was fun, he's a real charmer," yawned Rachel. "Norman too. Boy, he's really changed. But you know what? We still don't know why they're here. How come your letter didn't put Brillig off? Do you know where this is going?"

I had to admit that I too was in the dark.

---

[50] Ibid., par. 126.

3

An Unveiling

I awoke at 5:30. That's about when I usually get up. Even when there's not much to do, I like to get a jump on the day. Some weekends I force myself to sleep in, but that Saturday morning my mind was seething. In spite of all the drink—I think between us we finished four bottles of wine and fully half the Napoleon brandy—my head was clear as a bell.

Arnold was asleep on the couch with Sunny. She snooked an eye and closed it. I crept past them and put on a pot of coffee.

To my surprise Brillig emerged from the basement.

He was nattily attired in a brown suede vest with gold snaps, an open-neck shirt and those penny loafers stylish in the fifties. A thin silver chain circled his neck.

"Pardon me," he smiled, "I am an early riser, it is a good hour for exploring."

While he inspected my wall-hangings, I put the coffee and cups on a tray with a basket of sweet rolls and croissants, butter, strawberry jam and honey.

Brillig turned away from the French doors to the garden. It was still dark outside.

"You have published a good many books," he said.

I beamed. They were piled high in the basement.

"Why only Jungian analysts?" asked Brillig. "Do you think they have a monopoly on the truth?"

I heard Arnold stirring. Sunny padded in and licked my feet. I let her out in the garden and scooped food into her dish.

"It's pragmatic," I said. "There are only two of us. We couldn't cope with a flood of manuscripts."

I outlined the work involved—invoicing, packing, accounting, foreign rights, mailing lists, marketing and so on.

"And that's where your energy goes?"

"Yes," I said. "I have a few analysands, but otherwise I'm involved with the books. I work away in my room and send stuff into the world. Every morning at eight o'clock I go down to the post office to see what comes back. So far it's been a fair exchange."

Brillig nodded, as if he already knew.

I added knives and spoons to the tray and led the way upstairs to the sun room, Sunny at our heels.

We munched in silence, overlooking the garden, as dawn broke. There was a slight sprinkling of snow on the deck. Ice had formed on the plastic blanket covering the pool. The lone raccoon I called the Garden Bandit crouched forlornly on the fence. Black squirrels played hide-and-seek among the cedars. Two cardinals perched in the maple. Sunny rested her nose on my foot.

Brillig began to speak of his past life.

"While still quite young," he said, "I had already experienced virtually every pleasure and disappointment, every happiness and every suffering which can befall a man. I could give you chapter and verse, but the details are tiresome to any but me and ultimately of little consequence. The repertory of possible happenings in a human life is fairly limited; it is enough to recognize the pattern. Suffice to say that one day I found myself completely disaffected, a victim of high living and what I thought of as the holy trinity of the North American ethic: ambition, competition, success.

"I had entered the work force with an energetic zeal not uncommon among my generation, added to which was a desire to lead a meaningful and productive life. In short order I found that there were precious few outlets for its fulfillment. In those days it was child's play to make a living. Anyone with a half decent education could do it. For my part, I yearned for 'something else,' but I had no idea what that might be. Is this, I asked myself, what turns men into hermits, vagrants, sheltered academics, mystics, artists? Of lucre there was no lack, it flowed like water from golden spigots, but food for the soul was harder to come by.

"I quit the teaching post I held in a small town and journeyed to the city. I was appalled to find it even worse. I'm sure you know the opening lines of Rilke's *Notebook of Malte Laurids Brigge:* 'People come here, then, to live? I should rather have thought they came here to die.' I took this as my credo. Never mind that Rilke was a Dane in Paris and I was not. I too had been on the streets. I had been through the mill and knew it all to be a gigantic hoax.

"I took to siding with the underdog—the have-nots, the will-nots, the outsider. Fortunately I had a substantial legacy, for it was an expensive habit."

"And that's when you went to Zürich?" I asked.

"Oh goodness no," said Brillig, "this was long before. At that time, like many others, I had never heard of Jung. Indeed, there was no Institute until years later.[51]

"For a time I fancied myself as a writer. I tossed off several plays, two full-length novels and a bushel of self-righteous poems. I produced a large quantity of screeds, social polemics, which I hawked in the market. 'What a lot of progress there is,' I cried, 'and how it defeats itself!' 'What a lot of sterility, and how it multiplies!' 'Did you ever wonder,' I harangued perfect strangers, 'why there is Something instead of Nothing?' That sort of thing.

"Few listened. On the street I garnered sympathetic looks and the odd coin, and from publishing houses a few dozen rejection slips. I didn't have what it took, the right stuff.

"I became increasingly restless. I traveled, first to Europe, then to India and on to the Far East. I studied some improbable subjects, learned several trades, became fairly fluent in a number of languages. I fell in love with a few cities, some women and more than one man, but I did not find my rightful place, my 'home.' I know now that others had, and still have, the same problem, but with the arrogance typical of youth I felt unique. And very, very lonely.

"On the whole, I felt life was dealing with me somewhat like any vital organism treats a foreign body: it would either overwhelm me or shoot me out the back end."

"The poor me syndrome?" I said.[52]

"Yes," nodded Brillig, "I had a surfeit of it."

He replenished his plate.

"For a while, I believed I had found that 'something else' in religion. I became attached to a humble monastic Order headquartered in

---

[51] The Jung Institute in Zürich was established in 1948. Until then, becoming a Jungian analyst was a process of apprenticeship.
[52] This is outlined in my *Secret Raven: Conflict and Transformation in the Life of Franz Kafka,* pp. 97-98.

the Catskills. The name does not matter, you will not have heard of it. It was heretical, to say the least, with roots in the Gnostic tradition. The way of life suited me, for I was seeking surcease from the materialistic world—the avarice, the joyless pursuit of pleasure by waves of unthinking people who, in Nietzsche's words, 'register their existence with a dull astonishment.' "

I looked at Brillig, for I had used that very line myself in one of my books.

"Eh? You like that?" he smiled. "But perhaps you prefer parson Kierkegaard's bizarre query—'Which is harder: to be executed, or to suffer that prolonged agony which consists in being trampled to death by geese?' "

I laughed, recalling it from Brillig's thesis.

"In the monastery," he continued, "I found release from all that. I loved everything about the cloistered life—strict discipline and holy matins; solitude, chanting, regular chores and simple food.

"After acquitting myself as an acolyte I applied for, and was granted, a foreign posting. Along with several others I was sent across the sea, to Carpathia."

I started. "Kraznac? Chicken Little?"

"The same general area, yes, but rather closer to the Hungarian border. I was there several months before I became aware of her, except, as you will appreciate, by implication: it was the late thirties, storm clouds were forming; the end of the world—well, as we knew it—was in the air. Which is to say, the archetype of Armageddon was constellated. I had several apocalyptic visions similar to those Jung had before the First World War, but of course I didn't know that then.[53]

"It was in Upper Kraznac that I first heard of Ms. Little by name. Upper Kraznac was a bustling market town. Several Brothers—drawn by lot, for it was a privilege to be released from daily chores—journeyed there weekly for provisions. On mules it was six

---

[53] See *Memories, Dreams, Reflections,* p. 175: "I saw a monstrous flood covering all the northern and low-lying lands between the North Sea and the Alps. . . . I realized that a frightful catastrophe was in progress. I saw the mighty yellow waves, the floating rubble of civilization, and the drowned bodies of uncounted thousands. Then the whole sea turned to blood."

hours there and back. After we had made our purchases we were free to wander the streets and stalls for an hour or two before setting out to return.

"On one of these trips I chanced into a dingy little shop that apparently specialized in precious stones and antiquities. The merchant was eager to show me everything. I let him rattle on until he produced what he declared to be his prize possession: a small piece of lignous rock, roughly an inch square, with curious markings the like of which I had never seen. I inquired as to its origin and he proceeded to tell me the story of Chicken Little.

"Of course he knew much less of the facts than do you and I, for he was illiterate and his knowledge was no more than had been passed down to him through generations of peasants by word of mouth. You know how these things become embroidered in a predominantly oral culture. Perhaps because of all that, his account was especially vivid. I was immediately entranced. I must pursue this, I thought.

"Seeing my interest, the merchant pulled me into a corner.

" 'Sir,' he said, in that conspiratorial way that is so ubiquitous in the marketplace that one might call it archetypal, 'I have more.' "

"Whereupon he disappeared behind a tattered curtain; a moment later he emerged with a small leather pouch, out of which he spilled perhaps a dozen similar shards.

"The effect on me was remarkable and hitherto unknown. In light of my subsequent knowledge I would have to say the experience was numinous. It seemed to me that those small stones emitted an eerie light. They glowed.

"I was desperate to have one. Alas, I was penniless. Our Order adhered to a strict vow of poverty and we were allowed no funds of our own. The coins we returned with were always scrupulously matched with the cost of the vittles. Thus, when the merchant turned aside to serve a group of soldiers, I seized the opportunity."

I looked at Brillig with my mouth full.

"Simply put," he said, "I stole one."

I almost choked.

Not, certainly, at the confession of theft—I am no stranger to the shadow—but at the thought that he might have in his possession one of those very tablets "still to be found"—in the phrase I'd so blithely tossed off in my paper.

My mind was full of questions, but Brillig was in full flight and I was loath to interrupt.

"Had I lingered," he said, "I would surely have been caught. However, I was able to slip out, smiling and bowing, murmuring my thanks, before the merchant could realize what I'd done. I dashed back to join the other Brothers and we returned to our mountain retreat without incident.

"Alone in my room, I gloated. I tucked the stone under my pillow and spoke of it to no one.

"Some few weeks later we were hastily evacuated, first to Warsaw, then via Hamburg to Rotterdam, where we embarked on a freighter bound for New York.[54] I later learned that the area we had left, including both Kraznacs, was totally destroyed in an Allied bombing raid the following month."

I shook my head at this close call, but did not comprehend its full import until later in the day.

"From New York I returned to the home base of my Order, but I stayed only a few months, due to a pernicious custom that had been instituted in my absence. Every morning Father handed to each of us—we were about twenty in all—a slip of paper folded twice. One of these slips bore the words 'You're It'—meaning that the Brother so designated, unknown to anyone else, would play the part of Lilith all that day. Only Father knew who had received it. Perhaps on some days all the slips were blank, but, since no one knew, the result was the same, as you will see."

It was now getting on for eight. I heard someone entering the bathroom. Sunny left to see what was up.

I scratched my head and looked at Brillig.

"Lilith? . . . The legendary first wife of Adam? His devilishly sensuous mate before Eve?"

---

[54] This truly frightful journey in the shadow of troop movements and fleeing peasants is here passed over lightly. Brillig's extensive notes at the time, which Norman is in the process of editing, will be included in *The Compleat Brillig*. In the meantime, interested readers will find the flavor of such a trip dramatically captured in Sigrid McPherson, *The Refiner's Fire: Memoirs of a German Girlhood*, pp. 101ff.

"That is Hebrew folklore," replied Brillig. "According to other Semitic traditions, Lilith is simply an evil spirit who habits lonely places and takes possession of men's souls. Psychologically, I suppose, it amounts to the same thing: the personification of Dionysian ecstasy, unbridled lust."

Brillig paused and helped himself to another roll. He buttered it and spread a dollop of honey.

"I know of some rather horrible savage rituals," he continued. "Indeed, I have witnessed a few among certain primitive tribes— human sacrifice, cannibalism and so on. But in no religious sect or elsewhere have I ever encountered so cruel a custom as this institution of the daily Lilith.

"Imagine twenty determinedly pious men living communally, entirely deprived of female company, already half crazed by impure thoughts, knowing that one of their Brothers in Christ had been specially sanctioned to test the strength of their celibate vows—the breaking of which was punished by instant dismissal.

"To the constant terror of sinning was added suspicion. It was truly diabolical. Moreover, it did not even achieve its end. Furtive acts of venery still took place, only now it was like playing Russian roulette. You never knew which Brother was 'It.'

"I need not dwell on the extent to which this fiendish practice encouraged shadow projections and the severe repression of the anima. Of course, I did not think in Jungian terms at that time, but these are well-known features, by any other name, of virtually all fanatical religious groups. Let me speak rather of what was to me the worst aspect of this custom, namely, that not one among us ever refused to accept the role of Lilith. No one, when his turn came, had the slightest doubt that he was up to playing the part.

"More than once, I am ashamed to say, I too accepted the role of *agent provocateur.* I caught several, though I could not bring myself to turn them in.

"This all came to a head, and occasioned my leaving the Order, the day I realized the trap we had all fallen into—that the designated Lilith was himself the victim of a monstrous temptation, namely, to dredge up from within the most lascivious side of himself and to activate its counterpart—or 'hook,' as we now call it—in his neighbor.

In truth, of course, the one was no more guilty than the other. Until then I had always spotted those second-hand Liliths. They were so naive, always trying the same flirtatious tricks, poor mincing devils. They were simple fellows, after all, quite lacking in subtlety or imagination.

"Then came the day when I was caught off guard. A jolly new recruit, rough-hewn with big blue eyes, strolled up to me in a secluded grove during a rest period.

" 'The devil take this hair-shirt!' " he said congenially. " 'It doth irritate my privates.' "

"Whereupon he loosened his regulation suspenders. By the time his bottom was exposed I was half out of my britches.

"Suddenly I stopped. 'This is ridiculous,' I thought."

I smiled. Brillig laughed.

"I trust you understand that I had, and still have, nothing against homoerotic love. Indeed, I have always encouraged and respected warmth between men. It was the shoddy exploitation of this natural urge that suddenly struck me. In the time it took this beefy charlatan to rehitch his braces and forge a sanctimonious smirk, I was already stomping off to see Father.

"The head of our Order was not a bad man. We had had many intimate talks and I respected him. The worst I can say of the old fellow—he was close to eighty—is that he was ignorant, or, in retrospect, unconscious. Although I always felt him to be a faithful servant of the Almighty, he was directly answerable to anonymous higher-ups in Rome, obliged to enforce whatever cockamamie directives they saw fit to hand down. He was in no position to question them, nor indeed—and fortunately for him, I suppose—was he inclined to.

"He heard me out, as I knew he would. He clasped his hands and bowed his head. I saw his honest effort to think.

" 'My son,' " he said finally, " 'There is in you an incurable need to understand. This is not a desirable trait in our Order, nor can it be satisfied within it. I release you from your vows. We shall pray that God calls you to Him by other paths.'

"That night I packed my bags. I kneeled by the bed, for I was still devout, and asked God's forgiveness. Looking up, I pleaded,

'Show me the way.' Overcome by emotion, I imagined God defecating on my head."

"Something like Jung's vision?" I asked, moved.[55]

"Very much so," said Brillig, "only in my case it was certainly chicken shit."

"Holy cow," I said.

"Well," said Brillig, "that was it, my epiphany. In that moment I knew what was meant by grace. God was *not* dead.[56] Nor was he out there, *he was inside.*"

"But . . . but the droppings came from above," I pointed out.

"Only figuratively speaking," said Brillig. "Nothing actually fell on me. It was a vision. It all took place in my head."

"I see . . ."

"Most of all, perhaps, I felt an enormous relief. Yes, I was sinful, but I was not alone. God was with me. And to prove his humanity, to let me in on his little secret, as it were, he graced me with a bit of his shadow. It was also the clue to my direction."

I raised my eyebrows.

"You see," said Brillig, "in all the turmoil since returning from Europe I had quite forgotten the piece of stone I had run off with in Upper Kraznac. Struggling to make sense of my vision, I suddenly saw the connection and dug it out of my trunk. I kissed and fondled it and swore to honor its mystery.

---

[55] Jung's vision came to him at the age of twelve, while he struggled with dark and sinful thoughts. He imagined God sitting far away in a clear blue sky on a golden throne, judging him. He prayed to know God's will, then realized that God was testing him and he must think for himself:

"I gathered all my courage, as though I were about to leap forthwith into hell-fire, and let the thought come. I saw before me the [Basel] cathedral, the blue sky. God sits on His golden throne, high above the world—and from under the throne an enormous turd falls upon the sparkling new roof, shatters it, and breaks the walls of the cathedral asunder." *(Memories, Dreams, Reflections,* p. 39)

[56] Brillig was alluding, of course, to Nietzsche's famous remark in *The Gay Science:* "God is dead." In a subsequent conversation not recorded here, Brillig said that years later, after reading Jung's *Answer to Job,* it came to him that Nietzsche's declaration was never meant to be taken literally, but was merely foreseeing the decay of the traditional concept of God, "due [said Brillig] to more and more people withdrawing the projection of their inner divinity onto an external authority."

"In one way or another, Ms. Little has been a large part of my life ever since."

I lowered my head, feeling how frivolous by comparison was my own interest.

Brillig stood up and stretched.

"Cut loose from the monastery I slowly readjusted to secular life. During the war years I put aside my personal concerns. I was too old to be drafted, of course, but I did my duty on the home-front, working behind the scenes with various relief agencies.

"When the war was over I used my abilities to restock my diminished fortune. This was not difficult if you knew your elbow from your backside. Meanwhile, I resumed my search for meaning, immersing myself in what scholars now are wont to call 'the modern European mind.' That was when I discovered Jung. For some years he was only one among my many treasured 'guides,' but when once again I came to a dead end, I knew where to go."

He turned his face to the sun and fell silent. His profile was suffused in a golden light. A few wisps of white hair clung to his skull just above the ears.

The door opened and Rachel poked her head in.

"Pancakes and bacon in ten minutes. You guys interested?"

"Dear lady," smiled Brillig.

"We'll be right down," I said.

Rachel closed the door and I turned to Brillig.

"I am fascinated by the things you say, but tell me, why did you come? My letter was not exactly enthusiastic."

He shrugged.

"I read between the lines, my boy. Had you contacted me immediately—as I asked you to, my little trap—I would have been suspicious. I counted the days till your response. Every day I didn't hear from you was to my mind a plus. You were not to be easily lured. I liked that. When your letter arrived it was frank and to the point. I knew immediately that I had found a kindred soul. I informed you of my intention, giving you several days to call us off—just in case. You didn't.

"Meanwhile, I had obtained some of your other work. In truth it is an odd collection."

I felt a twinge of hurt. Seeing my crestfallen look, Brillig was quick to modify his words.

"Pardon me, I didn't mean to insult you; rather the opposite, for your writing does not denote one faint of heart. We need not pretend, man to man, that it is all good, but it was immediately clear to me that you have followed your daimon, as it were, whatever the cost."

Brillig now seemed more gnomish to me than ever. I looked at him with a feeling close to adulation. Had he asked me, I believe I would—and could—have walked with him on water.

"And so, you see, by the time Norman and I arrived on your doorstep I had deduced a comprehensive, though tentative, profile of what makes you tick. Our evening together confirmed it.

"Of course, with all due respect for your excellent company, I would not be here except for my long-standing belief in the existence of other Kraznac tablets. Until now I have been frustrated in attempts to prove this. But the very fact that there are now two of us changes everything. The task doesn't simply become twice as easy; *after having been impossible, it has become possible.*

"It's as if one set out to measure the distance from a star to our planet, with only one known point on the surface of the earth. It can't be done, of course; one needs at least two points, and then the distance can be found by triangulation."

I was completely bemused and could find nothing to say, except:

"But Norman—surely he too believes."

Brillig smiled.

"Norman? It is difficult to say. I think he would like to, but his education and typology mitigate against it. He is not comfortable in the world of abstract thought, nor does metaphor come easily to him. My impression is that Norman is waiting to be convinced. Meanwhile, he is along for the ride, as they say. For all that, he is a good companion. I have also brought him for practical reasons; as you will see, he has skills that could prove useful."

Fixed by those clear dark eyes, I felt I would believe anything Brillig said. My belly rumbled, as if to concur. If ever I had come across one who had achieved what Jung called "personality,"[57] this

---

[57] "Personality is the supreme realization of the innate idiosyncrasy of a living being. It is an act of high courage flung in the face of life, the abso-

man was it. And yet, at the same time, I imagined the reaction of friends and colleagues to an account of the conversation that had just taken place.

Rachel might appreciate it, and maybe Arnold too, but from others I could readily hear sarcasm, cynicism, perhaps even pity. I feared their searing wit, their scorn. Crowding out my instinctive esteem were such phrases as "gimpy old coot," "unfrocked monk," "daffy inventor," "not playing with a full deck."

Brillig touched my arm.

"Come," he said, "let us not keep the others waiting."

---

lute affirmation of all that constitutes the individual, the most successful adaptation to the universal conditions of existence coupled with the greatest possible freedom for self-determination." ("The Development of Personality," *The Development of Personality,* CW 17, par. 289)

4

Search for the Self

After we'd cleared away the remains of breakfast, Brillig spread some papers on the dining room table. I was relieved to see they were not maps of mountains. Walk on water, yes; climb to a great height, no.

Before sitting down to eat, Norman had pulled me aside and said he wanted to apologize.

"Whatever for?" I asked.

"I was really nervous about meeting you again," he confessed, "what with never writing and all."

I admitted to having occasionally wondered about him.[58]

"I've always felt a little guilty about not letting you know what happened. Last night I couldn't get to sleep for thinking about it. You saved my life and I've often had occasion to recall your words. I wanted you to know that."

I told him not to sweat it, it was enough to have him back.

"And your wife . . . Nancy?"

"Oh, she finally married a plumber. We're all great friends."

Now Brillig paced the room, lips pursed, rubbing his hands. His brow was deeply furrowed and I fancied the sound of great gears grinding. He'd asked if there was an easel he could use. Rachel found an old one of hers in the crawl space off the third floor and it was set up near the window.

Norman had opened one of their cases and was rummaging in it, putting things aside. He was singing to himself. I caught a few lines, which sounded like: "Here a little, there a little, everywhere a little little." My attention was then captured by Brillig rapping a pencil on the table.

---

[58] This was a face-saving understatement. The truth is that I spent months hoping to hear from Norman, and when there was no word I went into a severe depression. This had never happened to me before, nor has it since.

He struck a stance that I imagined dated back to his earlier days in a classroom.

"Gentlemen, Ms. Rachel," he said, "we all know there are many ways to look at the story of Chicken Little. On occasion I have fleshed these out, as has our friend here"—smiling at me—"but what is the central point, the nub, as they say?"

My brain was still somewhat addled from our earlier tête-à-tête; I couldn't come up with anything. Rachel shook her head.

After some moments Arnold spoke.

"That it's apocryphal?"

I looked daggers at Arnold, but Brillig only laughed.

"Dear sir," he said, "we live on one side of a mental curtain, in an age where anything one cannot see, hear, touch or taste is more or less apocryphal."

Norman nodded. "A corollary of the Brillig Principle."[59]

Arnold made what seemed to me a petulant gesture. Brillig noticed it right away.

"My friends," he said, "excuse my little self-indulgence, I did not mean to turn this into a guessing game. The fact is, Chicken Little personifies that fear lurking in us all, namely that the jig is up, we've had it."

"She was certainly pessimistic," noted Rachel.

"Dear lady, when gripped by the shadow of death, who can jump for joy? Only the very young, who feel immortal, and those who heed nothing. I call them closet Chicklers: they know the end is coming but they refuse to acknowledge it. The rest of us are stuck with the truth: we are mortal. Life is simply a prolonged stay of execution. Whether it ends naturally or with a sudden, arbitrary swing of the Scythe, one day we will be dust.

"As we know, it is the most natural thing in the world to project this awareness outside; which is to say, rather than put our own house in order, we imagine the world itself is coming to an end. That, I believe, is essentially what Ms. Little did and it is what regularly happens, especially when we lose someone close."

No one gainsaid him.

"Jung spoke of such matters, though rather obliquely," said Bril-

---

[59] See above, p. 37.

lig. He turned to Norman, who was ready. Brillig took the open book and read:

> There is a fine old story about a student who came to a rabbi and said, "In the golden days there were men who saw the face of God. Why don't they any more?" The Rabbi replied, "Because nowadays no one can stoop so low."
> One must stoop a little in order to fetch water from the stream.[60]

I did not know what to make of this, but there was no time to ponder, for at that point Brillig produced the stone of which he had spoken in the sun room.

Actual size

We gathered round for a close look. At first sight it was not impressive, indeed quite ordinary, but within a few seconds it seemed to glow. My mind turned to jelly. I stepped back, befuddled, and busied myself with Sunny.

Brillig gave Arnold and Rachel a brief account of his sleight-of-hand in the marketplace, already indelibly etched in my mind as the Carpathian Caper. No doubt Norman had heard it before.

"Only later," said Brillig, "after considerable research, did I realize that I had one of the few Kraznac tablets, if not the only one, outside the Smithsonian where, as we know, the others have been safely stored in an air-conditioned vault since 1908."

Arnold and Rachel fingered it, apparently unaffected.

"Who else knows about this?" asked Arnold.

"Only those in this room. I have been reluctant to speak or write about it before having more to say. As I remarked last night, there is a time for everything."

"How do you know it's genuine?" asked Rachel.

---

[60] *Memories, Dreams, Reflections,* p. 355.

"A sensible question," said Brillig. "Of course, there was no guarantee that I hadn't been duped. For all I knew, that merchant had a kiln in the back yard and turned them out by the hundreds. I had to consider that possibility. As well, I may have gulled myself. One man's numinous experience, as we well know, is another's wishful thinking. On both counts, I assure you I spared no effort in discovering the truth."

He then explained at some length how he had verified his catch. I was still in such a state that I could not follow all the details, but it amounted to a close comparison of his stone with the seven genuine articles under guard in the Smithsonian. This was not easily done, for a covenant with the donors—descendants of the monkish Order whose member had made the original find—specifically restricted access to accredited archaeologists.[61]

"I called in a few markers," said Brillig.

Arnold left the shard to Rachel and sat back.

"Professor Brillig," he said, "clearly you are a man of some intellectual discernment. I am therefore at a loss to understand your preoccupation with matters that to many—and I confess to leaning in their direction—might seem rather trivial."

There, he was at it again.

It was just like Arnold to get me into something and then shift his ground. One time in Zürich, on a pub crawl, he convinced me that the ugly one would be more interesting. The next day I showed him where she bit me.

"It's your own fault," he said, "you should know better."

I rolled my eyes at Brillig. He winked at me and addressed his remarks to Arnold.

"I could remind you of what Jung got out of playing with stones, so to speak,[62] but under the circumstances your comment is not entirely unfair.

"Perhaps I have given you the wrong impression. I am certainly concerned to uncover the truth about Ms. Little, but that is inextrica-

---

[61] That is still the case. The claim in my Chicken Little paper—to have seen "authenticated replicas"—was a bare-faced boast. They were really Xeroxes of covertly taken photos of hazy, dimly lit objects.

[62] See *Memories, Dreams, Reflections*, p. 175.

bly linked with a much larger issue—one in which you may have somewhat more interest."

"Namely?" pushed Arnold.

But Brillig was not to be hurried. He looked past us through the French doors and contemplated the falling snow. Huge flakes fell and glistened, melting on the glass.

"Rather early for snow, isn't it?" he said.

"That's what the papers say too," said Rachel.

I blinked, for the exchange was eerily familiar. I had the growing feeling that Brillig was to some extent prescient; more, that at times he was speaking in some secret code that only the two of us could understand.

"I have always thought of snowflakes as messages from heaven," said Brillig. "Like Iris, that sweet-tempered goddess of the rainbow, who brings a light we only dream of."

He turned back to Arnold.

"I could tell you that what I have in mind could lead to, among other things, the discovery of a law governing the behavior of feathered bipeds unable to conceive the number π . . . But I fear that something of that scope would stretch your credulity to the breaking point. I might just as well stand on my head and recite a verse or two from one of the masters."

Which he proceeded to do:

'Twas brillig, and the slithy toves
    Did gyre and gimble in the wabe:
All mimsy were the borogroves,
    And the mome raths outgrabe.

Beware the Jabberwock, my son!
    The jaws that bite, the claws that catch!
Beware the Jubjub bird, and shun
    The frumious Bandersnatch![63]

Rachel smiled across at me. Arnold was nonplussed.

Righting himself and making some adjustments to his clothes, Brillig became serious.

"Well, we could banter all day," he said, "as I do with the slow-

---

[63] Lewis Carroll, "Jabberwocky," in *Through the Looking Glass,* p. 22.

witted fellows I work with in factory and store—much to our mutual entertainment, to be sure. However, that is not what we are here for, and our time is short. Pray listen somewhat longer before you pronounce me a fool."

Arnold reddened.

"My great pleasure these past many years," said Brillig, "and my major preoccupation, of which Ms. Little has been a small but integral part, has been the scholarly investigation of that elusive concept known as 'the self.' Of course, this is tied up with what is to me, as I recall alluding to last night, the central question of life, namely, 'Who am I?'

"This query has haunted me for as long as I can remember. What does it mean when we use that extremely personal pronoun, 'I'? How very hard it is to grasp, this idea, this feeling, of 'I'! Indeed, there often seems to be more than one 'I,' for 'I' am not the same with different people, in different places—or alone. Could there be a common denominator? If not, perhaps there is a 'me' in this who holds us all together?"

He let that sink in and then continued.

"In the beginning, my studies were not concerned with discovering the truth or otherwise of what others thought was at the bottom of our sense of personal identity. Rather I sought out those thinkers and writers whose idea of the self was more or less central to an understanding of their work. There are a great many, as you know, and I was quite at sea until I focused on just three: Jean-Jacques Rousseau, Soren Kierkegaard and D.H. Lawrence.

"These illustrious gentlemen piqued my interest precisely because they were apparently as diverse as could be: Rousseau, eighteenth-century French paranoiac; Kierkegaard, nineteenth-century Danish religious introvert; and Lawrence, twentieth-century English iconoclast. Indeed, the only thing they seemed to have in common was an interest in exploring the implications of their particular understanding of 'the self.'

"I was easily able to characterize Rousseau's notions as pertaining to the *natural* self; Kierkegaard's were clearly related to the *religious* self; and D.H. Lawrence's stories and poetry illuminated what I thought of as the *vital* self.

"I also saw that their concerns overlapped."

Brillig paused then and grasped the back of a chair. I could not tell if he was about to do a hand-stand or was simply gathering strength. I did wonder if at his age he was really up to this.

Presently he inquired as to the possibility of some water. I ran to fetch a glass from the kitchen. Brillig thanked me and wet his throat before going on.[64]

"Rousseau and Kierkegaard were opposed to most of the values upheld by their contemporaries in the name of 'progress.' Both viewed material advance as evidence of—and factors contributing to—moral and spiritual decline. According to Rousseau—whose thinking was of course much influenced by the prevalent eighteenth-century ideal of the unfettered 'noble savage'—society was an evil influence that denied a person's self-realization in accordance with his true nature.[65] Instead of following the dictates of his own inner promptings, he lamented, man had become a slave to his social self.

"Kierkegaard, out of a similar concern for personal authenticity, deplored the influence of 'the crowd,' and what he called variously the leveling process or the tyranny of equality."

He took the book Norman handed him and read:

> To battle against princes and popes is easy compared with struggling against the masses, the tyranny of equality, against the grin of shallowness, nonsense, baseness and bestiality.[66]

"For Rousseau, it seems, salvation lay in a withdrawal into oneself, the tapping of so-called natural resources. Kierkegaard too saw the fulfillment of the individual as strictly a private affair, but he challenged men to become individuals 'before God,' by which he meant accepting the implications of what was involved in becoming a Christian. 'The whole development of the world,' he wrote, 'tends to the importance of the individual; that, and nothing else, is the principle of Christianity.'[67]

---

[64] During the following dissertation, as it seemed, he had frequent occasion to do the same, and I was quick to refill his glass as necessary.

[65] I trust my readers will not cavil at Brillig's use of the generic "he." There are still many who use it without disrespect for women.

[66] *The Journals of Soren Kierkegaard,* entry no. 1317.

[67] Ibid., p. 116.

"Dear old D.H., on the other hand—and what a handsome fellow he was!—saw personal growth and vitality in terms neither of self-absorption nor in a direct relationship with God. To be sure, there is in his view of nature and natural forces something akin to Rousseau's peculiar brand of mysticism,[68] but Lawrence believed emphatically that everything, even individuality itself, depended on human relationship.

" 'What are you,' " he demanded, " 'when you've asserted your grand independence, broken all the ties, or "bonds," and reduced yourself to a "pure individuality"?' And his unequivocal answer is echoed in much of his work: 'Extremely little!'[69]

"All the same, Lawrence—like Rousseau and Kierkegaard—was critical of the actual society he lived in. While believing in the necessity of communion with others, he too cautioned against the dangers to the individual self inherent in what has traditionally been called the civilizing process.

"In a broad sense, I saw all three as 'rebels against reason,' for each was opposed to the contemporary mainstream. Not that they denied the importance of reason or spurned its use. On the contrary. But each in his own way questioned the assumption that reason *per se* is man's most precious asset: Rousseau by attacking social institutions; Kierkegaard by stressing the primacy of faith and subjective truth; and Lawrence by proclaiming the potential vitality in renewing contact with a 'lower' consciousness.

"Each in his own time, you see, was an odd man out, a dissenter from a collective climate of opinion that had its roots in the Enlightenment and which to this day, I believe, determines the nature of Western society."

The discerning reader will have heard in the foregoing, as did I, echoes of Brillig's earlier revelations in the sun room. I do not mind saying that at this point tears sprung to my eyes. I was filled with an entirely new feeling. I could think of no name for it—something be-

---

[68] "The element of organic union is strong in both," said Brillig later, "but Rousseau's approach to nature is gentle, almost sentimental, while Lawrence seems to embrace nature with a fervor approaching physical lust."

[69] "We Need One Another," in *Phoenix: The Posthumous Papers of D.H. Lawrence,* p. 189.

tween mystery and hope.

I looked at Arnold and Rachel. They were motionless. Bored? Enthralled? I could not tell. Norman had left the room. Sunny was asleep in the corner.

For another half hour or so, Brillig continued to expound on the differences and similarities between these three "king-pins," as he called them, turning now and then to Norman, who provided him with a text to quote from.[70] Sometimes he used the easel to support a book to which he referred, though I believe this was merely for show, since as often as not it would be upside down.

"For a long time I put all my efforts into a comparative study of these gents, with only an occasional foray into the work of others. It was a thrilling enterprise until the day finally came when I realized I had no ground of my own.

"I knew what others thought I was or should be, but now the old question, 'Who am *I?*' came back with renewed vigor and grabbed me by the throat. I succumbed then to a severe and lengthy depression, during which time I became familiar with Jung. Only then did my research assume a psychological dimension, and considerably more depth."

Here Brillig took a healthy swig from the glass at hand.

"Gentlemen, I think you know what I mean. I needn't spell out to you the many ways in which Jung was balm to my troubled soul. Suffice to say, in terms of my personal quest, that his fundamental distinction between Self and ego was an eye-opener, for it is a distinction that everybody else either blurs or doesn't make at all. I was astounded at the idea that what I had always thought of as 'I' was merely the dominant complex of my conscious mind; and moreover that this 'I' was both answerable to, and dependent upon, a greater, transpersonal power, namely the Self."[71]

Arnold stirred. To his credit, he had been quiet for over an hour. Of course, he may have nodded off; you never know with Arnold.

---

[70] This account is deliberately abbreviated, since an edited transcript of the complete oration (which Norman had the foresight to tape) will appear in a later volume of Brillig's collected papers.

[71] Jung originally capitalized Self when using it in this sense, as do I, in order to distinguish it from the mundane ego-self.

"You would like to say something?" said Brillig.

"Jung's Self is as close to God as dammit," said Arnold.

"Yes, in terms of experiential reality," agreed Brillig, "but of course the traditional idea of a Supreme Being places him, or it, somewhere 'out there.' Jung's Self, as regulating center of the personality, is inside."

Norman handed him a book, from which Brillig read:

> The self is not only the centre, but also the whole circumference which embraces both conscious and unconscious; it is the centre of this totality, just as the ego is the centre of consciousness.[72]

He looked at Arnold and me.

"I won't presume to know how anyone else has reacted when they've come upon Jung's views, but to me they were extremely radical. To accept them meant a major shift in my perspective—like thinking the earth was the center of the solar system and then finding out the sun is."

"To begin with, for I was still tied to my research, I looked up everything Jung had ever said about my triumvirate. I was surprised, and more than a little disappointed, to find that they had hardly caught his attention. The references are few."

He paused to consult his papers.

"From Jung's standpoint, 'Rousseau is deceived,'[73] while Kierkegaard ('that grizzler')[74] is neurotic, if not actually a psychopath,[75] and furthermore lacks 'meat.'[76] D.H. Lawrence, whose *Weltanschauung* seemed to me to be close to Jung's own—for both had a high regard for personal experience and the 'instinct for life'—is never mentioned by Jung at all.

"I don't mind telling you that this occasioned in me some mental distress. But that's to put it mildly. Let us call it by its real name: conflict. The difference between what I had hitherto believed and what was presented to me by Jung threw me into a . . . a tizzy, I

---

[72] *Psychology and Alchemy,* CW 12, par. 44.

[73] *Psychological Types,* CW 6, par. 123.

[74] *Letters,* vol. 1, p. 331.

[75] Ibid., pp. 331-332.

[76] *Letters,* vol. 2, pp. 102, 145.

think is an appropriate word, and that's how I came to have a limp."

Rachel looked at me. I shrugged.

"No doubt you know the Biblical soap opera of Isaac and his sons Esau and Jacob. How the duplicitous Jacob stole his brother's birthright and became a rich merchant who regretted his past? And then wrestled with an angel? . . . Ah, I see you have forgotten.

"Norman?"

Brillig took the Bible and read:

> And Jacob was left alone; and there wrestled a man with him until the breaking of the day. And when he saw that he prevailed not against him, he touched the hollow of his thigh; and the hollow of Jacob's thigh was out of joint, as he wrestled with him. And he said, Let me go, for the day breaketh. And he said, I will not let thee go, except thou bless me. And he said unto him, What is thy name? And he said, Jacob. And he said, Thy name shall be called no more Jacob, but Israel.[77]

"My own experience was similar," said Brillig, "though not nearly so cosmic. But like Jacob I held on to my inner turmoil until I knew its meaning. I emerged from it humbled and thoroughly convinced of a presence more powerful than my puny 'I.' I could have dismissed the whole thing, I suppose, were it not for the difficulty I subsequently had in walking. I took it to heart and changed my name from Boris to Adam, for I felt reborn."

He stopped speaking, perhaps as much for our sake as his. I saw tears in Rachel's eyes and hid my own emotion behind a hanky. Brillig went on as if he hadn't noticed.

"That was some forty years ago. . . . My, time does roll along! Well, when I came out of my black hole—or dark night of the soul, as some call it—I realized that what Jung brought to my research was immeasurably greater than any mere belief, opinion or personal prejudice. First, he had sixty years of professional involvement with the human mind. And second, he awakened me to a dynamic model of the psyche, of which the Self is not only the regulating center but also the archetype of wholeness.

---

[77] Genesis 32: 24-28, King James Version. The psychological significance of Jacob's tussle is dealt with at length in John Sanford, *The Man Who Wrestled with God,* pp. 41-47.

"It became clear to me that beside Jung the others—including, alas, the three close to my heart—fell far short. Indeed, the primary limitations of every other commentator on the subject—and I think this is still true—were two-fold. First, they did not discriminate between ego consciousness and the unconscious; and second, they did not take into account the difference between the 'I' that bespeaks a socially-conditioned persona and a potentially more authentic 'I' behind it. This is not to mention the added nuance of the 'I' who nightly participates in dreams.[78]

"Of course, there was also the matter of conflict, which everybody else sought utopian ways to get rid of, while in Jung's view—amply supported by my own experience—conflict was extremely positive in terms of the relationship between the higher Self and what we think of as 'I.'[79] We needn't, I think, go into that today."

It was early afternoon as Brillig concluded an historical sketch of depth psychology—from shamanism to the present—with a thumbnail analysis of Jung's profound theoretical differences with Freud and Adler.[80]

"I trust that by now," he said, "the analogy between my pursuits and those of the alchemists will be obvious."

He pulled a large red and white handkerchief from his trouser pocket and blew his nose.

"I thank you for being attentive," he bowed.

He drained the water in his glass and abruptly left the room.

No one said a word as we followed the sound of Brillig's halting steps mounting to the third floor.

Sunny heaved to her feet and shook herself. She ambled over to Rachel, begging for a scratch. I looked at my notes and wondered if they'd make sense later.[81]

---

[78] There is a section on this in James A. Hall, *Jungian Dream Interpretation: A Handbook of Theory and Practice* (pp. 107-108), a book Brillig may well have chanced upon in his early morning jaunt in the basement.

[79] See *Memories, Dreams, Reflections,* pp. 344ff.

[80] Much of Brillig's source material was familiar to me, being readily available in Henri F. Ellenberger, *The Discovery of the Unconscious: The History and Evolution of Dynamic Psychiatry.*

[81] They didn't, but I didn't need them anyway, thanks to Norman's tape (see above, note 70).

"I expect he's going for a nap," remarked Norman, putting things away. "He tires easily these days, you know."

"You could have fooled me," said Rachel.

I looked at Arnold.

"He's either completely mad or a good actor," said Arnold, shaking his head.

I didn't think these were mutually exclusive, but I took it to mean he had some doubts.

"Well, I was impressed," I said.

"How about a sandwich?" asked Rachel brightly. "Rare roast beef smattered with peppercorns and horseradish? Sour dill pickle and white radish on the side?"

I was full up to here, so I left them snacking in the kitchen while I went out to clear the driveway. What had started some hours ago as a cheery fall of light flakes had become something close to a raging blizzard. It wasn't anything out of the ordinary, and the contractor I paid would soon be here with his plow. I just felt like some exercise after sitting for so long.

What a lot to take in, I thought, shoveling first to one side, then the other, while Sunny ran around in circles, snarfing up snow.

Car-dio-vas-cu-lar, I chanted, to pass the time. It was heavy work, but quite exhilarating.

Brillig's monkish background and literary interests; Kraznac, Chicken Little, Jung, the Self . . . and alchemy? God, the man must have a mind of steel to hold onto his sanity.

And then, beating away at a knotty piece of ice, I suddenly saw how they were all connected. Talk about epiphany. Everything fell into place. I tossed the shovel aside and leaped for joy.

"So happy to be a tomato!" I hollered.

I threw snowballs at Sunny and she threw them back. Next week, I thought, I'll teach her how to make a snowman.

Intermezzo

Two notes on the influence of Kafka

The Greeks regarded a problem like an apple: peel it, strip away the outer skin, the inessentials, and you come to the core, the solution.

But life itself is a whole basket of apples. The difficulty is to recognize the proper apple, to particularize life's problems. A man may spend years, indeed a whole lifetime, working through a basket, hopes rising as he nears the bottom, skins and cores piling up on all sides, only to realize at last that it is but one of many, there still await hundreds more baskets of apples, to say nothing of all the pears, bananas, peaches and oranges that he never thought of.

*

You arise one morning and wish to mail a letter. But the nearest post office is in a village several miles away. The sun is hot and the road to the village is over a tortuous rocky way, impassable at this time of year, beset with all manner of spring floods and other natural hazards. It is quite impossible, in fact, to reach this village, not with all the good will in the world nor a complete lifetime to spend in the journey.

If, however, by some unlikely chance, by some fantastic stretch of the imagination, and although it has never been known to happen before, you should eventually come to the village, it would certainly be after dark and already the post office would have closed for the night. And if you were to wait until the next morning, although there are no inns, hotels or guest houses where you could find shelter for the night, when the temperature falls far below the level at which anyone has ever been known to survive, you would find when you presented your letter to the postmaster that there were no stamps. Indeed, not for many years, and not within the memory of a living soul in the entire village, have there ever been any stamps at this post office; and you would have to send to the nearest town, the road there being even more hazardous and unlikely of navigation than the way to the village.

But that is only the first step, for application must be made at the town and sent to the city for inspection by the proper authorities, who are already overburdened by a thousand matters of more importance, unable to deal with even the most routine administration of the city itself, let alone the countless applications that flow in and pile up from all the towns and villages.

And if your children or your children's children happened to be still alive when, contrary to all expectation, your request finally did come up after all for consideration, they might perhaps hear that a stamp was on the way. This is by no means certain, however, since there is no instance, not a single occasion in all the records of all the villages, when anyone has ever received a stamp from the authorities.

It is said that this might explain why people don't get the letters they expect.

BOOK TWO
Star Bright

Alchemical library and laboratory
(Maier, *Tripus aureus,* 1618; Mellon Collection, Yale University)

"The double face of alchemy, laboratory and library, corresponds to the twofold nature of the individuation process: the active participation in outer reality and relationships, together with the process of inner reflection."

—Marie-Louise von Franz, *Alchemy, An Introduction.*

5
Philosophers' Stone

It was after six before we were back together. In the meantime, I had been home to change.

D. was still shoveling snow when I left, whooping and singing like someone demented. It's nice to see him happy; he's usually so serious and he works such long hours. Every morning he's down at the P.O. box like his life depended on it. I'm not making fun, because for all I know it does.

Norman waved good-bye from the bookcase. I nudged Arnold—he'd gone straight back to the couch after lunch with a detective novel—and he just snorted, which was typical. D. says Arnold's mother complex is of the negative kind—unlike D.'s own, I'm glad to say—and that makes him suspicious of women. Well excuse me, I never done him no wrong. I don't actually dislike Arnold, but I can't say I've ever been fond of him. I wouldn't be surprised if he feels the same about me, though looking for feeling from Arnold is like waiting for a peach to speak. I mean zee-ro. I don't know what D. sees in him, but then it's not really my business is it, and anyway some of my friends drive D. up the wall as well. I guess I put up with Arnold because he's D.'s friend. So maybe vice versa and that's all right too. The three of us get along when we have to.

I took Sunny with me, to give her a long romp in the park I live across from. She gets really down unless she has a good run about twice a day. It's always a thrill to see her race around, sniffing her little heart out, peeing at every tree and post. I meet a lot of interesting people that way; I don't always know their names but I recognize their pooches. It's such a friendly neighborhood, so different from the posh area D. lives in. A lot of people on my street are immigrants—Italian, Chinese, Indonesian, Portuguese and so on; even some Americans. There are three *bocce* pits and a playground in the park. We have a block party every summer, with races and games for the kids; pot-luck plates of food on trestles and dancing till midnight. On D.'s street they hardly know who lives next door. Still, he's close to good shops and restaurants. Together we have the best of both worlds.

Walking Sunny gives me time to think. I do like my life. I revel in my house, my own time and space. I feel so free to explore whatever catches my fancy. My painting has gone into an exciting new phase and I'm often so preoccupied I forget meals. News about the world makes me sick. I read in the papers about all the disasters and tear my hair. Television's worse. My heart sinks at the sight of starving children. I sign petitions to protect endangered species, send money for orphans, give to local food banks. It's never enough and I always feel guilty. So many people with nothing and I have so much. I'd be a hopeless wreck without my art.

I'm glad D. doesn't feel neglected. I suppose that's because he has his writing. Once he said he hoped I didn't feel left out when he was absorbed with a new project. I told him what's to worry, that's companionship; when I'm inside a painting I get lost too. Sometimes I get so excited I want to do it all at once but of course it's one step at a time and I forget half my ideas. D. says it's the same with him when he's working on a book. It's so different from any other relationship I've had that I want to shout it in the street. I feel understood. We accept the way the other is; like I don't expect too much of him when I throw a party, and he doesn't get on my case for the time I spend on the phone. We're different, no doubt about that, but it doesn't get in the way. He's an early riser and I'm not. He jokes about me being more extraverted, but as a matter of fact I'm quite happy to curl up with a book for a couple of hours when he packs it in at ten o'clock; and let me tell you, when he gets going he's the last to leave the dance floor.

Maybe the best thing about it is that we respect each other's boundaries. We're together, oh, three or four evenings a week, and that's enough. We both like time on our own and we both have things to do. It's not as cozy as togetherness, but it's not as sticky either.[82] Gives us a chance to miss each other, too.

---

[82] Actually, I used this comparison in *Getting To Know You* (p. 88), but I don't mind Rachel repeating it. Maybe it was even hers in the first place.

I'm not sure what to make of this "romance" he's gotten us into. Chicken Little's been a laugh to me from day one. D.'s paper had me on the floor even before he added my two cents worth. But now look how it's ballooned. I think D.'s a bit nervous about where it will take him; he can't stand insecurity and likes to stay put. He says if it was up to him he'd live in a hole and only come out to eat scraps thrown to him.[83] Sometimes I think a change would do him good, but then, I like my life as it is too. Come to that, I was attracted to D. in the first place because he was grounded. I was fed up with men who were up in the air. D. said he'd been there and it wasn't that much fun. He thinks maybe that's why he doesn't like heights—if he lets himself go he'd be in outer space again in a twink. So no wonder I was surprised, when the professor said he was coming—as if he'd been summoned with open arms!—and D. let it happen. Well, I just hope he can hold it together because I'd hate to lose him.

I can only imagine what went on this morning in the sun room. D. came down to breakfast looking like someone who'd fallen in love and wasn't quite sure what to do about it.

All the same, it's gone pretty well so far. Mind you, it isn't anything like what I expected, but I did enjoy last night. D. puts on a pretty good spread when he wants to. Norman's a real surprise. He's a lot more solid than when he used to come to D. I always thought of him as a klutz, a loser; he snuck in and out like he thought he was some kind of leper. M'am this and M'am that, when all I did was give him a cup of tea, which he proceeded to spill on his pants. Personally I've always been drawn to older men, the less hair the better. D. hasn't got much either, it runs in the family.

Brillig's a funny old guy, but there's an air about him that's hard to resist. I like his scent, *Old Must* I think it's called, though I may be wrong, there are so many out there you can hardly open a magazine these days without falling over your nose. He's kind of tricky, like one of those characters you read about in folklore; just when you

---

[83] This isn't quite what I said. I think Rachel misunderstood a passage I read to her from Kafka: "At bottom I am an incapable, ignorant person who if he had not been compelled to go to school would be fit only to crouch in a kennel, to leap out when food is offered him and to leap back when he has swallowed it." *(The Diaries of Franz Kafka, 1910-1913,* p. 308) I haven't felt that way myself since I got together with her.

think he's going to reveal the secret of life, he turns into a rabbit. But any eighty year old who has the chutzpah to recite poetry standing on his head will get my vote.

I got back a little later than I'd planned. I stretched a couple of canvases and started a new etching, then Sunny forgot where she lived and I spent half an hour looking for her. She finally slunk out of a back alley covered in snow and the smell of fish. She knows right away when she's been naughty. D. greeted me at the door with a jolly big smile and even Arnold gave me a hug. I suppose they'd had a few, but that's no big deal to me. D. said he'd spent a couple of hours correcting page proofs and clearing up correspondence, with Norman in a corner browsing through my portfolio. D. has a few pieces of mine in his office, including a self-nude you wouldn't see in a family newspaper—"so you're always with me," he says. I like that. Intimate at a distance.

The four of us were gathered around the fireplace in the living room when Brillig made his entrance. He was freshly showered and his goatee had been newly trimmed. So he likes to look his best, well who doesn't; I don't mind a degree of vanity, it shows self-respect. He was dressed in khaki shorts and a bush shirt, long woolen socks and lace-up mountain boots. On his head was one of those Tilley Endurables you see in ads of people on top of sand dunes or beside Land Rovers in the Alps.

D. gave me a weak smile, pointing to his knees. I couldn't tell if he was pretending or if they were really shaking at the possibility of an expedition.

I blew him a kiss and would have jumped him then and there if we'd been alone.

"Yes, certainly," said Brillig briskly, responding to Arnold's invitation. "A glass of claret frees the soul. The frenzied followers of Dionysus didn't know the half of it," he laughed. "Tearing people to pieces isn't nearly so satisfying as loving them."

The old guy seemed in pretty good form; I guess a little rest was all he needed.

About seven the doorbell rang. It was a delivery. Dear D., always planning ahead. He'd ordered a buffet tray of assorted meats and cheese, smoked salmon, cognac paté, oysters, cabbage rolls, Caesar salad, rye bread, sweet biscuits and a Bavarian chocolate mousse. You can't do much better than that; well, I couldn't. There were even a couple of beef bones for Sunny. D. and I set it all out so we could help ourselves when we felt like it.

For a while I got stuck with Norman and Arnold, trading stories about their escapades in the Niederdorf. Drinking and screwing—borrr-ring. You'd think they had the I.Q. of Turkey Lurkey. I mean who cares? I've been around too, I could tell stories of my own, but what's the point? You only give yourself away.

I was half listening when the corner of my eye caught D. showing my sketch book to Brillig, dangling his feet like an elf in one of D.'s leather armchairs. I went over to find them looking at the drawings I'd done of us.

Brillig smiled up at me.

"Miss Rachel," he said, "you have a remarkable talent."

I glowed with pleasure. The thought came to me that if Brillig was half my age, or me twice mine, I'd show him a good time. It was an amusing thought, but pretty surprising too, because it didn't fit my image of myself. Well, what can you do. D. says you're not responsible for everything that goes on in your head, only for what you do about it. So maybe he has fantasies of his own. All the same, it seems pretty dumb to think of hopping into bed with somebody just because they like your work.

Norman came and peered over my shoulder.

"I look like Sam Shepard," he remarked.

"That's how I see you," I said, "handsome in a weathered way."

"How come I look like a gangster?" asked Arnold.

Brillig said it was absolutely the best likeness of himself he'd ever seen, and might he possibly have a copy to take home and hang in his study.

"I seldom find myself in such compatible company," he said. "At my age you like to have a record of what's important. Please, do me the honor of explaining how you are able to capture one's inner essence with such grace."

Talk about a cup overflowing.

Conversation was lively, though more or less random, until D. asked Brillig what he'd had in mind when he compared his work to that of the alchemists.

"Well, as you know," replied Brillig, "alchemy was the chemistry of the Middle Ages, ostensibly concerned with the transmutation of base metals, particularly lead, into gold. Interestingly enough, it is sometimes spelled 'alchymy,' derived from the old French, which in turn comes from the medieval Latin 'alchemia' and the Greek 'cheem,' meaning to pour."

I didn't think that was particularly interesting, but maybe it's like painting: you have to start somewhere. Getting from here to there isn't as simple as it looks after you've done it.

"It was Jung's genius," Brillig was saying, "to discover in what's been called the holy technique of alchemy a parallel to the psychological process of individuation.[84] In those old Greek and Latin manuscripts he found the same images and motifs that turned up in myths and legends, as well as in people's dreams. He felt right away that he was on to something important, and so he was, for his investigations eventually led to his discovery of the archetypes.

"What it comes down to is that the alchemists—obliged to work under wraps, incidentally, due to some rather nasty restrictions on free thought imposed by the Church—were really looking for emotional balance and wholeness. Not much different from the rest of us, is it? Which is to say, the secret art of alchemy lay in the transformation of the personality. I have always taken this to mean that anyone involved in his, or her"—bowing to me—"psychological development is an alchemist, so to speak. Norman?"

Norman hadn't been paying much attention—bless him, he was brushing Sunny—but now he scrambled and came up with a book to hand to Brillig, who read:

> The real nature of matter was unknown to the alchemist: he knew it only in hints. In seeking to explore it he projected the unconscious

---

[84] This awareness informs all Jung's mature writing, but his three major works in the area are *Psychology and Alchemy,* CW 12; *Alchemical Studies,* CW 13; and *Mysterium Coniunctionis,* CW 14. For those who find Jung intimidating, a good place to start is Marie-Louise von Franz, *Alchemy: An Introduction to the Symbolism and the Psychology.*

into the darkness of matter in order to illuminate it. In order to explain the mystery of matter he projected yet another mystery—his
own unknown psychic background. . . .

> . . . I mean by this that while working on his chemical experi-
> ments the operator had certain psychic experiences which appeared to
> him as the particular behavior of the chemical process. Since it was
> a question of projection, he was naturally unconscious of the fact
> that the experiment had nothing to do with matter itself . . . . He
> experienced his projection as a property of matter; but what he was
> in reality experiencing was his own unconscious.[85]

"Early on in my acquaintance with alchemy," continued Brillig,
"my imagination was struck by the concept of the Philosophers'
Stone,[86] and how similar it was to Jung's idea of the Self. Psychologically, the Philosophers' Stone is an archetypal image of wholeness. I immediately realized, as you probably have, that the tablet I'd
snatched years before in Kraznac falls into the same category.

"Naturally, having in mind Jung's remarks, I had to take into account the possibility that the numinosity I experienced in that stone
was due to something in me. By then I knew the stone was genuine,
but what about me, was I authentic? What about the way I felt?
Could I trust that? It was a new context, but essentially the same old
question, 'Who am I?'

"Well, I took care of that little item, though it took rather longer
than I'd expected. In fact, the first two years of my analysis were
spent differentiating my ego-self from that greater Self, which I'd
identified with and then projected onto Ms. Little. That's about how
long it took for me to get a handle on personal boundaries—where I
ended and she began was only the start. My analyst, normally a pa-
tient man, was more than once obliged to remind me of the difference
between the Philosophers' Stone and a stoned philosopher."

---

[85] "The Psychic Nature of the Alchemical Work," *Psychology and Alchemy,*
CW 13, pars. 345-346. Those interested in the therapeutic application of alchemical thought will find ample reason to rejoice in Edward F. Edinger,
Anatomy of the Psyche: Alchemical Symbolism in Psychotherapy.
[86] "Make a round circle of man and woman, extract therefrom a quadrangle
and from it a triangle. Make the circle round, and you will have the Philosophers' Stone." (From the *Rosarium philosophorum,* cited by Jung in "Psychology and Religion," *Psychology and Religion,* CW 11, par. 92)

D. was busy taking notes. Arnold was cleaning his nails. Norman was sorting things.

"It was a humbling experience," said Brillig. "Indeed, 'deflating' would not be too strong a word, for it meant having to acknowledge my limitations. I was all blown up, you see; I thought of myself as somebody special, a common affliction of those who lack a psychological perspective, and symptomatic, as you well know, of that ubiquitous phenomenon we call the puer. Norman?"

He handed Brillig a tattered notebook.

"Here's something I wrote from a lofty height"—

Darwin's Applecart: There is no essential physiological difference between men and other animals.

Nietzsche's Ethic: Self-realization. Man has a unique position in the animal world because of his additional *potential.* Anyone may raise himself above the ordinary, the animal level, by cultivating his true nature: "The man who would not belong in the mass needs only to cease being comfortable with himself; he should follow his conscience which shouts at him: 'Be yourself! You are not really all that which you do, think, and desire now.' "

Accepting Darwin's view, Nietzsche recognized that the significant gap is not between ordinary man and the animals, who differ in degree only, but between ordinary man and that higher form of man who indulges in essentially human activities—art, religion and philosophy. This is the "supra-animalic triad" within which, claimed Nietzsche, a man may most fully explore his potential.

"Well, there you are," said Brillig, and stopped. He pulled his Tilley over his eyes and began to chant.

I didn't know what to think. A glance at D. and Arnold told me they were no better off. Norman was rocking on his heels, smiling. Sunny gave me a quizzical look and rolled onto her back, legs flailing; she does that when she doesn't know what else to do.

"I'm lost," I said, to no one in particular. *"Where* are we?"

Brillig peeked out one twinkling eye.

"Dear lady," he said, "I thought you'd never ask."

He stood up on the chair. Tossing his Tilley to Norman he did a little jig. Then he sat down and pulled his legs up so they almost circled his neck. Holding this position he spoke, so softly that I could hardly hear.

"Men deal with reality in any number of clever ways, all of which prove nothing. Reality is no challenge, exacts from man nothing more than the will to survive, which is possessed by the lowest animal. What is more important in the making of a man is how he copes with the *un*reality of his life, how he handles the abstract, the unknown, the merely possible.

"Here is where one's highest abilities are brought into play. Here is where the individual is separated from the group. In this area man explores the intellectual, philosophical and spiritual side of himself, contemplates the dark side of the moon, opens the atom, probes the microbe, seeks the very answers to life itself. The man who opens these doors transcends his own mortality in a very real sense. For behind them lies a compelling reflection of his own potential."

This was pretty exciting stuff. It seemed to me his eyes had taken on a, well, maniacal look. D. was mesmerized.

"You may recall the words of that eminent pessimist Céline: 'To philosophize is only another way of being afraid and leads hardly anywhere but to cowardly make-believe.'[87]

"Well," said Brillig, "it was no secret to me that he who would construct a world of dreams risks living in a nightmare. The more I had become concerned with ideas, the less tolerant I was of those immersed in what I considered to be petty things. The longer I sought the meaning of life, the reasons for it all, the more jealously I guarded my personal truths and the more vulnerable I became to the cruelty and harshness of the world.

"But, I asked, the man who seeks protection in himself, through philosophy, is he really a coward? While exploring his own sense of a deeper reality, is he not retreating, but, on the contrary, preparing to advance? Philosophy—which I was, and still am, inclined to characterize as the awareness of, and search for, 'something else'—is more than a day-to-day refuge from the humiliation it can mean to be a social animal. It is also the way in which one builds stepping-stones to the future."

Brillig unwound himself and beckoned to Norman, who threw his hat back. Brillig tipped it at D.

"Your friend Kafka showed me the way out of what threatened to

---

[87] *Journey to the End of the Night,* p. 126.

become a small box. Remember? 'Strange,' he writes, as if in answer to Céline, 'how make-believe, if engaged in systematically enough, can change into reality.'[88]

He stopped speaking and wiped his brow with his sleeve. I took the opportunity to offer him a cabbage roll. He thanked me and wolfed down two.

"Gentlemen, Ms. Rachel," he said gravely, "I swear to you, there is not one word of what I have just said that I really believe. That is, I do believe it, perhaps, but at the same time I feel and suspect that I am lying like a cobbler."[89]

I couldn't help it, I burst out laughing.

Brillig smiled at me.

"You get the point," he said. "The only trouble with philosophy is philosophers. As Jung said about improving education: it is first necessary to educate the educators."[90]

He paused, looking into space.

"I think it was not until my fourth year of analysis," he said, "that I realized there was nothing intrinsically wrong with the struggle to express an inner vision of a reality greater than the individual self, a reality that transcends the mundane. And I still believe that the struggle to understand and assimilate the essential nature of man is more important in the long run than, for instance, making money—but it's not real, it's *creative make-believe*.

"And that, dear friends, has become the governing principle of my life."

He stood up and stretched his little legs. Then he got down on all fours and crept up to Sunny. She licked his face and he licked hers. They grappled and almost rolled into the fireplace, which fortunately wasn't lit.

---

[88] *The Diaries of Franz Kafka, 1914-1923,* p. 210.

[89] This extraordinary admission is almost exactly the same as Dostoyevsky's wry comment in *Notes from Underground* (p. 36). I believe it to be an example of cryptomnesia, or "hidden memory," whereby something once known but long forgotten comes to mind, but without the original source (so that it seems to be one's own). See Jung, "The Psychology of So-Called Occult Phenomena," *Psychiatric Studies,* CW 1, pars. 138-148.

[90] See, for instance, "Analytical Psychology and Education," *The Development of Personality,* CW 17.

D. was looking pensive.

"What are you thinking?" I asked.

"I was trying to remember," said D., "something Aldous Huxley wrote."

He went to the bookcase and ran his fingers along the spines. After a moment he pulled out an old paperback.

"Here it is"—

Most men and women lead lives at the worst so painful, at the best so monotonous, poor and limited, that the urge to escape, the longing to transcend themselves if only for a few moments, is and has always been one of the principal appetites of the soul.[91]

"Yes," said Brillig, plucking off dog-hairs, "and that's certainly quite as true of me as of anyone else. But think of this: when you lose the impact and personal immediacy of your dreams and ideals, when you're no longer inclined, or able, to invest your mundane history with the grandeur of a personal evolution, then might you not just as well be dead?"

It came to me then that the old guy must have led a pretty lonely life. I said as much.

He inclined his head.

"Birds, animals, fish, and all manner of fruits and vegetables, have their prescribed cycles for growth and decay. They may be counted upon, with few exceptions, to adhere to a pattern as sure and predictable as the movement of the stars. One's art, on the other hand, is fitful and unpredictable; it cannot be relied upon at all. Or, as Rilke says, 'Friends do not prevent our solitude, they only limit our aloneness.' "[92]

There didn't seem much to say after that. My mind felt like a pretzel. It was late and it looked like everyone was tired. I took Sunny out in the snow for a few minutes. When we came back they were carrying leftovers into the kitchen.

Brillig was speaking to D.

". . . so I dare say you're right about that, since to my knowledge

---

[91] *Doors of Perception*, and *Heaven and Hell*, p. 16.

[92] *The Notebook of Malte Laurids Brigge*, p. 85.

you and I are the only analysts who are also bona fide Chickle Schtickers. The Jungian community does not, as a whole, care two figs about Ms. Little."

Arnold butted in.

"And why should they?" he asked impishly.

Brillig looked at Arnold as if he—Arnold—hadn't heard a word all evening.

"Because, my dear boy, Ms. Little holds the key to Jung's theory of the collective unconscious."

I looked at D. He didn't seem all that surprised.

"Come off it," laughed Arnold. "Chicken Little couldn't tell the difference between a cucumber and a milkshake."

"Somebody, please sit on his head," said D.

Norman laughed.

"In any case," said D., carefully packing the dishwasher, "it's not theory, it's fact."

Brillig gestured.

"Yes, yes, I agree, but the world doesn't. Even though the word theory derives from the Greek *theorein,* 'looking about the world,' somehow it has got round that Jung thought it all up in his head. People need proof. Indeed, I myself, with my penchant for facts, do too. Without facts, I can fall back on personal experience; lacking both, I'm as skeptical as the next man."

I had to speak.

"And just where do you think these facts will come from?"

He yawned.

"It's been a long evening. Tomorrow is soon enough. I bless you for indulging the ravings of an old man and bid you *bonne nuit.* Come, Norman, let us not outstay our welcome."

They went up the stairs hand in hand.

Arnold said it was getting so crazy around here that he was beginning to feel normal. He thought he'd go home where he'd be safe. D. said he hoped he'd come back in the morning. Arnold said he'd have to leave that to fate. D punched him in the arm and said how does it feel to have the tables turned, eh? Arnold grinned and said watch your step, there's a banana in your ear.

D. was restless in bed. Twitches and whimpers, teeth grinding. About three o'clock he sat bolt upright and said: "If Chicken Little were a man she'd be president of Procter and Gamble."

I pulled him to me and touched him where he likes. "Talk, talk, talk," I whispered. "I like it better when you *do.*"

He did. And I did.

6
A Stitch in Time

The singing birds, the flowers that open their eyes, each in their own season; childbirth, sickness, pain; like an enigmatic inscription I once found in a book— "Thu 9.00"—what does it all mean? What is it all for? The longest road, even in the long run, is usually longer than the shortest. That is obvious to most, though some may deny it. But that the longest road has the most delightful lanes, inviting towpaths, this is not so generally known.

Were every country lane to be swallowed up tomorrow, wiped from the face of the earth without a trace, birds would surely cease to sing, flowers would close their eyes, out of respect.
—Adam Brillig (from an old notebook).

Looks like the beginning of Creation out there. Must have snowed all night. The trees are heavy with white. Quiet, no traffic. I see the moon and can almost hear it. It's so cozy up here, I think I'll just stay under the covers until the sun comes up. One of these days it will be my last.

The attic suits me. How very different from years ago, when as a young man I thrived on the excitement of the street. You never knew who or what might turn up—just around the next corner. Anything was possible. That feeling kept me going in bad times. And when things didn't pan out the way I wanted, I tore off a finely crafted rant. In those days I imagined I could make a difference. I mingled, made speeches, directed committees; I was often the life of the party. All for nought. My pearls of wisdom, fresh off the press, fell like stools from a mule. I can't remember now why I thought anyone would be interested. Vanity, I suppose, what else.

My life then was little more than a show for others. Some of it still is, of course; you have to go through the motions or you'd be all alone. Well, I don't mind a few motions if that's what it takes. I couldn't do without solitude, but I like some company too; as long as

I can say where and when. I don't regret the past, what I was. But it's a long time since I had much interest in what goes on out there. So much fuss, so much noise; action and reaction. *Plus ça change, plus que la même chose.*

The only thing that matters to me now is what happens inside. Everything else is for the birds.

D.'s mice were out in force last night, scuffling in the walls. Very comforting. I shall recommend that he keep them. It took me back fifty years, to when I holed up in a tenement in London to write what I was pleased to think of as my next book. I'd bang the typewriter for hours, and when I ran out of steam I'd press my ear to the floor and listen to the rats. I imagined them stowing away old bulbs and seedlings for the winter. There'd be a flurry of feet, then silence— when I fancied they were listening to me . . .

> For now and then they stop awhile,
> Nothing much of value.
> It's not as if the place abounds
> In carrots, leeks and marrow.
>
> Oh, that the rot would not set in!
> I'd give a left or right arm
> To stop it crumbling to the ground—
> Quite a lot of value.

You forget so much if you don't keep tabs. How to distinguish one day from the next; by what yardstick to measure past sorrows and gladness; how to select from the dross of routine a stream of valid and significant recollections, memories not defaced in the retelling, experiences that retain their original glow when recounted to an unknown listener; how to recreate with truth and honesty the atmosphere of fading emotions; how to sift and separate, file and classify, the trivial, the important, the monstrous, the repercussions of a chance encounter, the implications of an unanswered invitation; how, in short, to relive a lifetime—that is the fate of the lonely, the old, the abandoned and the voluntary exile.

Like a drunken sailor who has missed his boat and finds himself marooned in a hostile port, that's the man who has cast away, or lost, his connections with the past.

I'd be writing this all down in my journal if I still kept one. It's where I always felt I came closest to the truth. I was ten years old when I started my first diary—a record of events, nothing more, but how I prized my secrets!—and sixty-two when I stopped. Over half a century of intimacy with myself, whoever that was. Then one day I realized I was hedging. Somebody's listening, I'd think—or should be. More vanity.

The unexamined life, said Jung, is not worth living. I do agree, I just don't write it down any more. Nothing lost, though, it's all stored in my head.

Come to think of it, is the unlived life worth examining? I don't know if Jung said anything about that.

"Professor Brillig?"

I opened an eye to see Ms. Rachel in a long velvet robe, holding a tray.

"Tea and cinnamon rolls," she announced. "I thought you might like something to hold you till breakfast."

I mumbled thanks.

She set the tray on the side table. Bending over, she brushed aside my night cap and pecked my bald spot.

How sweet. She does get my blood going. If I was half my age or she twice hers, I'd doo-wah-ditty.[93] Guess there's some spark in me yet. Not that I do much with it these days, but dear me I had a pretty good run. There was no getting away from it; what went up had to come down.

She was half out the door when I found a voice.

"I wouldn't mind . . . if you stayed . . . ," I said.

"Thought you'd never ask," she smiled, pulling up a chair.

There was an aura about her. Self-possessed, confident, thoroughly feminine. I clutched the covers to my chin. It was years since I'd been in such a situation. I didn't know quite what to say.

"Did you sleep well?" she asked.

"Peaceful as the damned," I said.

"Bad dreams?"

---

[93] This is so like Rachel's thought (above, p. 77) that I can't help seeing it as an example of how the unconscious flits about in time and space.

"Good, bad, who can tell? Lots of them, though. Haven't had a dreamless night since my head exploded, what, forty years ago, and I cried for three days. There were snakes last night, toads and . . . elephants? I forget."

Rachel poured some tea and buttered a roll.

"I do like your work," I said.

"Thank you, some people find it too erotic."

She stretched and yawned; her zipper slipped a shade and I began to feel something was up.

"My dear, art is art," I said. "The whole point of being an artist is the freedom to explore, to let your imagination go; that's where you find your center."

"Trust lust," she said.

We sipped in turn from the one cup.

"I dream a lot too," said Ms. Rachel, "but I can hardly ever understand them."

"Well, you're in good company. Jung said the same about his own dreams. There's no Archimedean point, no objectivity. That's what an analyst's for."

"I dreamt of you last night," she smiled, licking her lips.

"You did?"

"We were making love on a raft."

"Oh?"

"Under a cloudless sky in the middle of the ocean. . . . Now, why on earth would I dream something like that?"

"An heroic journey, perhaps . . . the sea of life . . . getting close to your inner man, your *yang* . . . that sort of thing. I'd have to know you better, and your associations to me."

"You're . . . special, I like you."

"How did you feel when you woke up?"

"Well, I can tell you, pretty excited. I'm glad D. was there. He got most of it."

I was wondering how much was left, when she slipped under the covers.

"Dear lady! . . . what about D.!?"

"Hush," she murmured, snuggling close. "There's not much difference between you and him. He has a little more hair, is all."

My fantasies, what would I be without them? And they, without me? Chicken Little, now, I wouldn't mind being quit of her, but she grips me so. Intransigent complex, obsession, *idée fixe,* whatever; I'm more interested in what it means than what it's called.

If I were fifty years younger and half as scrupulous, I'd start a religion. Or a cult, more likely. I'd aim to squeeze the poor and dispossessed, those most vulnerable. I'd hire someone with a commanding presence to go on prime time television in a black robe and cry out, HALLELUJAH!!! Ms. Little came to earth to save yo' SOULS! The sky was fallin' then and it still is! Don' you hear them clouds clappin'? Frien's, they is gettin' ready t' FALL!! An' when they falls, you don' wanna be unda them, do you? Now, how you gonna 'scape a fallin' cloud o' horror and hell-fire damnation? Well frien's, all you gotta do is BELIEVE!—man, woman 'n' chil', you gotta believe in the worda Ms. Little!! And jus' what's all that about, you ask, just what's this l'il Ms. Little got that you ain't got and ain't never had? Well, I'm here to tell ya what she got that you ain't; I'm here to tell ya WHAT SHE GOT that you ain' NEVER HAD. And that's SOUL! Brothers 'n' sisters, the soula Ms. Little is available to alla you, no single man, woman or chil' gonna go without. It's a BIG SOUL an' a piece of it's there for the askin'. All you gotta do is BELIEVE!—Come forth now, march right up, don' be shy, she loves ya all and nobody gonna be left out who truly BELIEVES! An' out there in the big wide worl', I hear ya, ya wanna come up the aisle like these true believers, on'y ya ain't here! So how you too gonna be saved? Well, I'm here to tell ya, ya gonna be saved jus' the same when ya send yo' MONEY! Ms. Little ain' no high hoss up on no hill; she ain' makin' you come to her, she gonna 'cept yo' true belief from WHERE YOU IS!! . . .

I couldn't do that now, of course. Thanks to analysis for that. It brought my chickens home to roost, so to speak. It put an end to all sorts of delusions, like the belief that I knew what I was doing; that I could survive alone; that I could grow, feeding only on myself; that I was particularly different. Hasn't all been roses, though. Lost a few angels as well as devils. Just when you get hold of a really good fantasy, reality hits you in the eye. Isn't that the shits. Still, I don't trip over myself as much.

The prodigal son. Once the myth got under my skin, there was no question about it, I had to return. But first I had to leave. My mother cried at the boat: "Come back and be one of us." I did go back, but not to be one of them. I let them watch me from a distance, bending here and there, picking up the threads of a finely-woven myth. Perversely, I would not stop until I had delivered it raveled.

The big question then was how to make freedom creative. Could I realize my potential by plunging head-first into life? Should I proceed with caution? Opt out? How to make a choice from the limitless possibilities—that was the biggest question of all, and to some extent it still is. The purpose of life could resolve the issue, but then what *is* its purpose? Jung believed the purpose of human life is to become conscious. Maybe that's true. But conscious of *what?*[94]

How little we know of all this. Born infants, we die as children, hardly mature enough to cope with ourselves, let alone lead whole nations. If we could live as long as Methuselah, at what age would we begin to profit from our mistakes? A hundred and ten? A hundred and fifty? When would we escape the familiar cycle of growth and decay and truly begin to evolve? At what age would we solve the mystery of our own existence?

Or is it not simply a matter of living longer to understand more? Do we reach a plateau, as Kierkegaard believed, where everything is reversed, after which the struggle is to realize that many things can't be understood at all? That's Socratic ignorance, he said: we continue to mature until we become children again.

Oh, I did love Kierkegaard's *Journals,* I could live on one of his nuggets for days.

"A life which is not clear about itself inevitably displays an uneven surface."[95]

---

[94] With all due respect, I am at a loss to understand how Brillig could have missed Jung's point, which is that consciousness is an end in itself, and moreover is useful: "The reason why consciousness exists, and why there is an urge to widen and deepen it, is very simple: without consciousness things go less well." ("Analytical Psychology and *Weltanschauung,*" *The Structure and Dynamics of the Psyche,* CW 8, par. 695) Jung's essential views on this subject are presented in Edward F. Edinger, *The Creation of Consciousness: Jung's Myth for Modern Man.*

[95] *Journals,* p. 47.

"One cannot reap immediately where one has sown. . . . One does not begin feasting at dawn but at sunset."[96]

"For the rights of understanding to be valid one must venture into life, out on the sea and lift up one's voice, and not stand on the shore and watch others fighting and struggling."[97]

"During the first period of a man's life the greatest danger is: *not to take the risk.* When once the risks have been really taken then the greatest danger is to risk too much. By not risking at first one turns aside and serves trivialities; in the second case, by risking too much, one turns aside to the fantastic, and perhaps to presumption."[98]

It was a piece of luck to chance on D.'s paper. I think they're hooked, at least he is for sure. Poor boy, he almost had a fit when he saw me in my safari gear. The others?—well, we'll see. I think there's a piece of Ms. Little in everyone; you just have to coax it out. I do hope it works because I could never pull this off on my own. All these years, looking for just the right mix. Of course they don't know what's in store, but all in good time.

Oh I do love secrets; they're the life blood of the soul.[99]

I'm now exactly three years older than Jung was when he died. I wish I could say I was half as wise. I don't feel old but I *think* old. I look old too, but I don't mind that. People make way and don't expect so much. The pressure's off. Well, from outside. There's always the inner heat, of course; once the fire's lit, you can't get rid of it. Who am I, indeed.

I think I'll wear the harlequin outfit today.

*

After breakfast D. asked my views on Ms. Little's typology.[100]

[96] Ibid.

[97] Ibid., p. 68.

[98] Ibid., p. 192.

[99] Jung thought so too. See *Memories, Dreams, Reflections,* pp. 342ff.

[100] According to Jung's model, there are four basic functions by which we orient ourselves in the world. Briefly, *sensation* establishes that something exists, *thinking* tells us what it is, *feeling* evaluates what it's worth to us, and through *intuition* we have a sense of its possibilities. See "General Description of the Types, *Psychological Types,* CW 6, pars. 556ff, and Daryl Sharp, *Personality Types: Jung's Model of Typology.*

"Well," I said, "there are many imponderables. I once thought she was a sensation type, for at least she knew she'd been hit. A weak thinking function could lead her to mistake a branch, say, for a piece of sky, and inferior intuition would tempt her to fasten on the dark possibilities. On the other hand, superior intuition could have alerted her to a bleak future others don't see—a skyless world, as it were. Or did a well-developed feeling function spur her to run off, so as not to risk getting hit again? Then there's the shadow, which distorts everything. In short, I'm disinclined to label anyone typologically, let alone Ms. Little, whose behavior patterns are so ambiguous."

Then Ms. Rachel brought up my remark yesterday about lying like a cobbler.

"I gather you meant it as a joke," she said, "but it's such an odd simile. In fairy tales shoemakers have a reputation for humility and integrity. They can be trusted."

"Good public relations, my dear," I replied. "The cobbling fraternity has made the best of an oft-repeated remark by Jesus: 'The last shall be first.'[101] Then there was that toad-in-the-hole Gepetto, who conned Pinocchio into growing up. Personally I have never been unduly impressed by those who work with animal skins. Their shadow is just as likely to take over as is anyone else's.

"Symbolically, of course, shoes are associated with the standpoint. 'If the shoe fits,' we say, 'wear it.' Taking a stand is said to be the measure of a man. To be sure, shoes, unlike feet, are not something we're born with. We can choose. At first our choices are guided by others, then by our own experience. Yet all through life, what fits one day may pinch the next.

"Take that Marcos woman, now—750 pairs of shoes, give or take a few. Some would say she has a problem—but perhaps she has the answer. The personality is not homogenous, it has as many facets as a diamond. Otherwise we'd know who we were right off the bat. We wouldn't have to wonder."

"Gepetto . . . ," said Ms. Rachel. "Wasn't he a carpenter?"

Trust her to catch that one.

"Watch it grow," I smiled, pointing to my nose.

Arnold burst out.

---

[101] E.g., Mat. 20:30.

"You mean you say things you don't believe?"

Really, coming from him this was laughable. Arnold is a born mocker, I knew it from the start. However, it's in my nature to take people at face value. They seldom know what they say, and generally I don't tell them what I hear unless they're paying; otherwise there's no fair exchange. So I answered impersonally.

"I wish it were that simple," I said. "I long ago realized that whatever I said, the opposite was equally true—or at least worth considering. Perhaps you will recall the way the ancient Greeks felt about the people of Crete—they were thought to be inveterate liars, but you could never be sure."

"Oh!" exclaimed D. "The Riddle of the Cretan Liar?"

"Yes, the same. One Cretan put it this way: 'I admit that I am a liar. Therefore nothing I say is true.'

"Naturally this begs a question or two. Was he telling the truth only when he lied? Or was his admission itself a lie and he was lying only when he told the truth?

"This malicious conundrum exercised the ancients for some centuries. It has survived to the present for good reason: it taxes the brain cells. Of course, the Greeks knew of only the conscious mind, which we now know is only a fraction of the whole. As Jung said, 'Consciousness does not create itself—it wells up from unknown depths';[102] namely, from the unconscious.

"Indeed, the real significance of the Cretan's confession—which to my mind is only exceeded by the riddle of the Sphinx[103]—is only apparent in light of Jung's idea of the shadow, whereby the good and honorable intentions of our right hand are continually being outfoxed by our left.

"I believe there are more than a few Cretans in my family tree, as I dare say there are in yours. Only an outright charlatan sets out delib-

---

[102] "The Psychology of Eastern Meditation," *Psychology and Religion,* CW 11, par. 935.
[103] See Jung, "Flying Saucers, A Modern Myth," *Civilization in Transition,* CW 10, par. 714: "How are you fulfilling your life's task . . . your *raison d'être,* the meaning and purpose of your existence? This is the question of individuation, the most fateful of all questions, which was put to Oedipus in the form of the childish riddle of the Sphinx and was radically misunderstood by him."

erately to deceive. The rest of us"—and here I looked pointedly at Arnold—"do it willy-nilly."

I turned to D.

"To whom was your paper on Chicken Little addressed? Did you write it for Jungians or Chickle Schtickers?"

He thought a minute.

"Either . . . no, both . . . maybe neither . . ." he fumbled. "Well to tell the honest truth, I don't remember."

"Exactly," I said. "The cobbler's children go barefoot."

There was more small talk, which I didn't mind at all. I was in no hurry. I enjoyed the company and I knew it wouldn't be long before I was on my own. I felt somewhat like a genie who'd been let out of a bottle: soon I'd be stuffed back in.

Yet there was D., getting restless. Funny thing about him, he says he likes things the way they are, but get him started on something new and he won't let go.

Finally he couldn't hold back.

"Professor Brillig, Adam," he said, "I don't mean to rush you, but you did say you knew the location of other Kraznac tablets."

"Indeed, and I do."

"And where might they be?"

I pulled the stone from my pocket and held it up to the light.

Dear Ms. Little. Normally a dull shade of mousy-brown, I had cleaned her earlier with salts of ammonia. She did gleam and her finely etched glyphs stood out like canyons.

"Here," I said, *"in potentia."*

D. gasped. Arnold snorted. Ms. Rachel wrinkled her brow.

I must admit I relished their consternation. My words hung in the air like balloons. The only sound was the soft, whistling escape of gas from the blessèd dog.

7
New Dimensions

Adam does love a little drama. If it had been up to me, we'd have got to this point the first night and be home by now. That's what I suggested on our way here. Give it to them straight, I said, no beating around the bush. Adam tsk-tsked and said the goal wasn't all that important, we might never get there; so let's just relax, he said, and enjoy the journey.

Well, it wasn't for me to say, was it? It was his idea, after all, and it's been his show from the beginning.

I'm not sure how I got into this. Chicken Little isn't really my cup of tea. I don't mind playing stagehand, though. Adam usually knows what he's doing, but even flying blind he's entertaining. He says he's an introvert; so then where does the showman come from? Persona? Shadow? Anima? Puer? I used to know the jargon. When I worked with D. he said it was important to give a name to my different parts—so they stop possessing you, he said. Well, it worked; at least I found my way. I owe D. a lot; it wasn't exactly his doing, of course, but he was there.

D. was so excited when I went off to Zürich. Maybe he was hoping I'd relive his past. I don't know; at the time I thought it was my own idea, but maybe I did go just to please him. Maybe that's why, when it didn't work out, I couldn't bring myself to tell him.

Shopping around for an analyst in Zürich was an interesting experience. The Institute handed out a list of about a hundred, with the languages they worked in. You picked a few and called them to set up interviews. And then you got together with other candidates and heard the gossip.

"Frau M. is hard of hearing. Speak softly and smile a lot."

"My analyst hardly says a word. I squirm but it works for me. I have to think for myself."

"Dr. N.? Let me tell you about Dr. N. He lives alone with a hungry Alsation. If she doesn't like you, forget it."

Dr. P. was my first choice, but I couldn't see him right away so I had a session with Frau B., just in case.

"*Ja*, you are lonely without your family, but who isn't? The question is what to do. Hmm? Hmm? We fix."

Dr. P. was a balding Englishman in his sixties. He had left a medical practice in England in 1950 and never went back. Left his wife, too. We hit it off right away. He was a lot like D.; I had the feeling he could empathize with my situation.

"What do you hear from your children?" he asked.

He had none himself, but he didn't flinch when I cried. I was sorry to leave him after only a few months, but it was clear by then that I wasn't cut out to be an analyst.

"Accept yourself," he advised. "You're more comfortable with the outside world."

Anyway, maybe I did grow up, more or less. At least I'm content now with what I've got. Before, I was always looking for something better; I only felt happy when I was stoned, floating from place to place, moment to moment. I went with the flow. I felt like a god and behaved like one. I shall never forget the exhilaration, the freedom, the clarity. But for what? I felt creative, but I didn't create. I felt beautiful, but did ugly things. I felt invulnerable, but I hurt a lot. I paid a high price for a meager return. I lost people I loved.

Meeting Adam may be the best thing that's ever happened to me. Sure, I like my work, but it's the relationship with him that matters. He's kind and gentle and for all his learning he never puts me down. He's so much older, and yet I feel we're buddies. His manner reminds me of what I read about an old monk in a book Dr. P. gave me when I left.[104] Sometimes I get the feeling Adam knows everything, but he seemed genuinely surprised when I showed him the books D. wrote about us. Then he got all fired up.

Maybe that's what's so satisfying about being with Adam—there's always something new. He can take off in a minute, but he always stays close to the ground and I never feel left out.

---

[104] This took some tracking down, as Norman had long since lost it. But while browsing through my stacks he recognized the picture reproduced opposite, which was used in von Franz, *Alchemy: An Introduction,* to illustrate the goal of individuation.

Entering the City with Bliss-Bestowing Hands
(the last of the "Ten Ox-herding Pictures" of Zen Buddhism)

"And now having moved through the stage of emptiness, and also having seen God in the world of nature, the individual can see God in the world of men. Enlightened mingling in the market place with 'wine-bibbers and butchers' (publicans and sinners), he recognizes the 'inner light' of 'Buddha-nature' in everyone. He doesn't need to hold himself aloof nor to be weighted down by a sense of duty or responsibility, nor to follow a set of patterns of other holy men, nor to imitate the past. He is so in harmony with life that he is content to be inconspicuous, to be an instrument, not a leader. He simply does what seems to him natural. But though in the market place he seems to be an ordinary man, something happens to the people among whom he mingles. They too become part of the harmony of the universe."—Suzuki, *Manual of Zen Buddhism.*

I was afraid I'd missed my cue, but the room was still enveloped in, well, a balloon of silence.

Adam was gazing at the snow through the French doors. Arnold was picking his teeth; D. and Rachel were examining the stone. I caught a whiff of dog-fart, but I wasn't about to embarrass Sunny by mentioning it.

When Adam turned to face us he spoke with unusual gravity.

"To the untrained eye," he said, "that insignificant piece of rock has no value at all. Yet to me it is alive."

He began to pace.

"Early in life I realized that for a proper appreciation of my own nature, and for a social perspective I sadly lacked, it was incumbent upon me to withdraw for a time from the mainstream of life—to take a step back, both symbolically and in fact, from the company of others. I learned thereby that the man who would be different has two battles to fight: one against the opinions of others, and one against himself.

"Remember Kierkegaard? 'To battle against princes and popes is easy compared with struggling against the masses, the tyranny of equality.'[105] But the struggle within can be equally as devastating. It took my all to counter the forces intent on bending me back into line. And if such pressures were often 'only' mental—subtle internal conflicts rather than flesh-and-blood antagonists—so much the worse; they were phantoms far more difficult to cope with.

"Never mind, what is done is done and no regrets. What I say to you now is that the shell I became was filled by Ms. Little, who in the guise of a stone embodied and summed up all my struggles. Objectively that was nonsense; subjectively it was so, because I invested it with elements of myself. More—the *best* of myself, what I wanted to be, might have been, never was or could be.

"Initially, as I intimated yesterday, the bond was so close that I *was* her; or, at least, she was my soul-mate and I was nobody without her. Some years of analysis took care of that. And then, having withdrawn my projection, what was left? Well, at first, nothing; I was bereft. But finally, a great deal more.

"In the first place, I got a little closer to who I was, myself, with-

---

[105] See above, p. 62.

out her, and secondly, I became intrigued by who *she* was, without me. In other words, I discovered the otherness of Ms. Little.

"I don't mind telling you that this has turned out to be incalculably more valuable than anything of myself I'd seen in her. It meant that I could actually have a *relationship* with Ms. Little—not just dote on her as a reflection of myself."

D. and Rachel exchanged smiles.

"To make a long story short, my attachment to the stone increased rather than diminished."

Arnold stood up and clapped, slowly.

"Well done, Prof," he said. "You replaced one fantasy with another. Pardon me for wondering why the second is any more admirable than the first."

D. groaned.

For a minute I thought Adam was going to stand on his head again—he's pretty good at that, I've only seen him fall once—but he took a more gracious tack.

"Sir," said Adam, "your skepticism is quite in order. Indeed, you have hit on the salient background to the erratic progression of my life: I am weak and I long not to be; I am little and long to be big; I am nobody and long to be known. I am besotted with Ms. Little and she is not available."

He conjured up a tear. He's good at that too.

"Between Ms. Little and a stone, others may see a considerable difference. But to my mind it does not amount to much. I relate to this tablet as to an abandoned child. To me, you see, on top of everything else, it represents the neglected Goddess, and thus compensates the patriarchal conception of the feminine as a mere trifle, something not worth bothering about."

"Bravo!" cried Rachel.

"Thank you," bowed Adam. "Let others call this a misguided fantasy, but like the stone the builders rejected—flung into the street like a worthless piece of dung—it has become the guiding light of my life—my personal Grail."[106]

---

[106] Brillig later confirmed that he was thinking of the Biblical "stone which the builders rejected, the same is become the head of the corner." (Psalms 118:22, Acts. 43:11; mentioned by Jesus in Mat. 21:42)

Adam crossed the floor and selected a book from D.'s shelf. He leafed through it, found a passage, then read:

Night after night our dreams practise philosophy on their own account. What is more, when we attempt to give these numina the slip and angrily reject the alchemical gold which the unconscious offers, things do in fact go badly with us, we may even develop symptoms in defiance of all reason, but the moment we face up to the stumbling-block and make it—if only hypothetically—the cornerstone, the symptoms vanish and we feel "unaccountably" well.[107]

"Outside of the alchemical *lapis,* the stone has quite a respectable pedigree as a Self-image. Incorruptibility, permanence and divinity are among its fabled attributes. I've done some research myself, but it pales beside the analogies Jung unearthed. Listen to this"—

The stone as the birthplace of the gods (e.g., the birth of Mithras from a stone) is attested by primitive legends of stone-births which go back to ideas that are even more ancient—for instance, the view of the Australian aborigines that children's souls live in a special stone called the "child-stone." They can be made to migrate into a uterus by rubbing the "child-stone" with a *churinga. Churingas* may be boulders, or oblong stones artificially shaped and decorated, or oblong, flattened pieces of wood ornamented in the same way. . . . The *churingas* used for ceremonial purposes are daubed with red ochre, anointed with fat, bedded or wrapped in leaves, and copiously spat on (spittle = mana).[108]

I looked around to see who was following this. Rachel smiled at me; D. was scribbling. Arnold was either feigning sleep or dead.
Adam continued reading:

These ideas of magic stones are found not only in Australia and Melanesia but also in India and Burma, and in Europe itself. For example, the madness of Orestes was cured by a stone in Laconia. Zeus found respite from the sorrows of love by sitting on a stone in Leucadia. In India, a young man will tread upon a stone in order to ob-

---

[107] "The Symbolism of the Mandala," *Psychology and Alchemy,* CW 12, par. 247.
[108] "The Visions of Zosimos," *Alchemical Studies,* CW 13, par. 128. (Mana is a Melanesian word referring to a bewitching or numinous quality in gods and sacred objects.)

tain firmness of character, and a bride will do the same to ensure her own faithfulness. According to Saxo Grammaticus, the electors of the king stood on stones in order to give their vote permanence. The green stone of Arran was used both for healing and for taking oaths on. A cache of "soul stones," similar to *churingas,* was found in a cave on the river Birs near Basel, and during recent excavations of the pole-dwellings on the little lake at Burgaeschi, in Canton Solothurn, a group of boulders was discovered wrapped in the bark of birch trees. This very ancient conception of the magical power of stones led on a higher level of culture to the similar importance attached to gems, to which all kinds of magical and medicinal properties were attributed. The gems that are the most famous in history are even supposed to have been responsible for the tragedies that befell their owners.[109]

"And on and on it goes," said Adam, closing the book with a snap. "From ancient times and in all cultures, the stone has represented something precious—an amalgam of body, soul and spirit. Only recently, of course, has psychological research shown that the myriad historical or ethnological symbols are identical with those spontaneously produced by the unconscious. Jung himself was the first to call attention to the fact that the *lapis* represents the idea of a transcendent totality which coincides with the Self."

He stopped speaking and I wondered if he'd gone too fast. It was rather a lot to swallow.

"I don't quite understand . . . ," Rachel said hesitantly. "How can a stone represent both the feminine and the Self?"

Adam was ready for that.

"Among the intriguing characteristics of symbols," he said, "is that they are paradoxical. Not exactly all things to all men, but certainly different things to different men—and women too, of course. You might care to rephrase your question to reflect this. For instance, 'When is a stone not a stone?'—to which the answer may well be, 'When it's something else.' "

"And Chicken Little," asked Rachel, "didn't you say the other night that she personifies the repressed side of God?"

"Yes," replied Adam, "but I believe the Zeitgeist is taking care of

---

[109] Ibid, par. 129.

that. Thanks in no small part to our mentor Jung, the feminine is coming to the fore as an essential balance to the traditionally masculine God-image—Yahweh's neglected opposite. What happens next, of course, depends a good deal on how conscious we become individually. Make no mistake about it, what we do and are has an effect on the great Him.[110] And I dare say the same is true of Ms. Little."

Rachel seemed perplexed. Perhaps she would have pursued it, but D. spoke.

"Look," he said, "this is all very interesting, but aren't we getting off track? The other tablets?"

"Very well," said Adam.

He shook his fool's cap, the one with bells. I'd begged him not to bring it, it makes him look ridiculous. Personally, I much prefer the miter, but it wasn't my call.

"Who knows something about holography?" asked Adam.

There, that was my signal. I readied myself.

Arnold shook his head.

D. shrugged, though I must say it was hard to imagine he didn't know what was coming.

"I've been to the Science Museum," said Rachel. "They have a laser show with flashing lights, and next to it there's a booth with some holograms. Oh, and I have one on my credit card."

"Holography," nodded Adam, "is a photographic technique for storing, or better say capturing, three dimensional visual information on a two-dimensional plane. I cannot claim to understand how it is done, but fortunately we have an expert with us—my helpful *frater mysticus.*"

He motioned to me and I took over, as planned.

"Holography," I said, "was conceived by the physicist Denis Gabor. Using a complicated white light source he made the first holograms in 1948 at the Imperial Institute in London. They were merely a curiosity until the invention of the laser in 1960.

"Most holograms are made with a laser—because it emits a continuous, monochromatic beam of light—using an inanimate object as the subject. They are viewed as though one were looking through a

---

[110] See Edward F. Edinger, *Transformation of the God-Image: An Elucidation of Jung's* Answer to Job.

window, with a transparent film or glass plate being the window. For the purposes of holography, one can think of the laser as simply a special kind of bulb emitting a single color of coherent light, which means light waves of the same wavelength moving in parallel at the same speed."

"To make a hologram, an unexposed photographic film, or glass plate, is set up facing the object in total darkness. Part of a laser beam illuminates the object, and the rest of the beam is deflected by mirrors to the film. The film receives the wave pattern of both the direct laser beam and the laser light reflected from the object. The result is an interference pattern which is recorded on the film. That's a hologram."

D. nodded. "This sounds familiar."

"When the film is developed," I continued, "it looks no more like a picture than a gramophone record or a cassette tape looks like music. But when it's illuminated by a monochromatic light source, the interference pattern enables the original holographed object to become visible in three dimensions. When you move your head, you can see 'around' the object, just as if it were there, right in front of your eyes.

"Early holograms were of the transmission type. To be viewed, they had to be illuminated with either laser light or a white light source which had been filtered to one particular wavelength. Most modern holograms—like those on credit cards—are of the reflection type; they can be viewed in ordinary light.

"Now, a major difficulty from the beginning was to create a vibration-free environment for everything involved in the making of a hologram—the object, the laser, all the lenses and mirrors and so on—because the film has to be exposed for several seconds. As it happens, this problem was solved by an artist."

I pulled a slim booklet from my pocket and held it up.

"You may recognize this," I said to D., and read the title: *"On Holography and a Way To Make Holograms."*

"Holy smoke!" exclaimed D. "Pethick wrote that over twenty years ago! I used to have a copy."

"You may recall, then," I said, "that it describes a simple set-up for making holograms in a sandbox. The box itself rests on an inflated inner tube, so nothing shakes."

Adam smiled at me—Pethick's book was our little surprise—and pointed at the shimmering creations we'd seen on D.'s walls when we first came in.

"He is the same man who did these, is he not?"

D. nodded.

"I would dearly like to meet him," said Adam.

"One day, perhaps," said D., "but not so easy, he lives on an island," and turned to me.

"Where on earth did you find it?"

"Quite by chance, actually. Two years ago I was passing through Peoria and stopped in to greet a used bookseller I know. He had come across it in a batch he'd bought. Knowing my interest in the subject, he had put it aside."

Rachel turned the pages with wonder.

"D., you never told me about this."

"Cripes," said D. "I'd forgotten about it myself."

Arnold coughed.

"Thank you very much for this cozy little display of old home week," he said, addressing us all. "To the bizarre exploits of a mythical chicken and the magical quality of stones, we now add an esoteric third dimension. I'm beginning to feel like I'm trapped in a loony bin."

What a strange duck is Arnold. He's as unpredictable as Adam. One minute he's hail-fellow-well-met and the next a devil's advocate. I didn't know what to say, but Adam gave him what for.

"My dear fellow," he said, "is your tongue actually forked or just tucked in your cheek?"

Arnold winced.

"Technology," said Adam, "has developed a host of new tools for those who are interested, but it takes time and talent to realize their intrinsic value. The application of holography to communications and the human environment may yet have a more far-reaching effect on our society than anything we can now conceive."

"Are we here to debate the future?" asked Arnold, still testy.

"Not at all," Adam smiled, "nor would I trouble you simply to indulge an old man's whim. The science of holography—from the

Greek meaning 'whole picture'—is directly relevant to our current pursuit. Norman, please go on."

If we get this far, Adam had said, it's all up to you.

"It is a curious fact," I said, "known to anyone working in the field, that if a holographic plate is broken, the original image can be recreated from any piece of the broken plate. The resolution isn't so good, of course, but with a series of optical filters designed especially for the purpose, the clarity can be boosted to something very close to the original."

"From a fragment?" asked Rachel. "A bitty piece?"

"Yes," I said, "it's all there."

"Hard to believe," said Arnold.

"And there I'm with you!" said Adam, clapping Arnold's shoulder. "But it's true, I've seen it."

"So have I," said D.

Adam nodded at me.

Now came the truly ticklish part. I spoke slowly.

"Given these basic facts," I said, "it is possible that under the right circumstances, and looked at in the right light, one might also discern a virtual image—in the aura of the hologram, so to speak—of what the object was once part of."

That was it, the end of my notes.

There was dead silence, during which I wondered if the significance of my little speech had sunk in.

D. stroked his cheeks.

"That isn't in Pethick's book."

"It is still a hypothesis," I admitted.

"What is a virtual image?" asked Rachel.

"Something that isn't really there," said Arnold laconically.

"True enough," I agreed, "yet we see it as if it were."

"Let me get this straight," said D. "Are you saying that a hologram of Adam's stone might provide a picture of the complete rock —the larger whole it was broken off from?"

"Yes," I said, feeling a sudden surge of belief.

"Precisely," said Adam. *"Recreate the past."*

Arnold held his head. "I think I'd like a drink."

D. looked at Rachel.

"Well, lover, what do you think? Is it a crazy idea?"

Adam had said earlier that if we could get Rachel on side, so to speak, we were home free. I could only imagine how he knew this, but I crossed my fingers.

"Strange, unlikely, yes," she said quietly, "but crazy, no."

"So you really take this seriously?" scoffed Arnold.

"More than that," said Rachel. "It may be the most serious idea I've come across in my life."

"Good for you!" said D., hugging her.

"Well now," said Adam, rubbing his hands, "Let us begin. Norman and I have brought the necessary equipment. All we need is a basement."

"We can use mine," said Rachel crisply. "It only makes sense, since D.'s is full."

D. turned to Arnold.

"C'mon, old buddy! Are you with us?"

Arnold scowled and threw up his hands.

"Oh, what the hell!" he said. "In for a penny, in for a pound."

8

The Experiment

It did not take long to transport the materials to Rachel's—she lived only ten minutes away—but setting it up was something else. That took all Sunday afternoon.

On the way over I was as anxious as I was excited. I was grateful to Rachel for her offer, but uneasy about leaving my container. While in my house, I could imagine this all taking place in my own psyche, with the players being aspects of myself: me, the ego; Arnold, *eminence grise;* Norman, lapsed puer; Brillig, mercurial trickster; and Rachel, part-time muse. A neat conceit—a manageable cast for self-discovery, assembled with considerable thought, under my control. There was even a place for Sunny.

But they did have lives of their own. At one remove, perhaps, but still. At any minute, any one of them—or, God forbid, all at once—might do something out of character.

What if old Brillig suddenly took it into his head to become a businessman?

What if Norman started spouting philosophy?

What if Arnold became less cantankerous?

What if Rachel cut me off?

And, the most disquieting possibility of all, what if I got to like it outside? *Who would "I" be then?*

I took some comfort in Jung's remark that "a life without inner contradiction is either only half a life or else a life in the Beyond, which is destined only for angels"[111]—but not much.

In any case, my own dilemma, if I can call it that, was quite secondary to the task at hand, namely to create a hologram of Brillig's piece of Ms. Little. How we got here, or why, was no longer important. I thrust aside my troubling thoughts and resolved to see it through.

---

[111] *Letters,* vol. 1, p. 375.

No team of mountain climbers set to with more vigor than did our little troupe. No expedition up the Orinoco was ever better prepared. It was absolutely astounding how much stuff was in Brillig and Norman's second trunk, which up till now had not been opened. Indeed, that they'd lugged it all this way I took as an extraordinary gesture of faith.

Rachel blanched when she saw the cables.

"Where's the main switch box?" asked Norman.

She recovered and showed the way.

While Norman busied himself with electrical connections, Brillig and Arnold positioned a large tractor tire inner tube in the middle of the basement floor. I inflated it with a bicycle pump they'd brought. Together we built a four-foot square box out of plywood, using two-inch blocks at the corners so the sides were a foot high, and covered the bottom with a thin layer of carpet material. A piece of wood was nailed along one edge of the box to hold the laser. We centered the box on top of the inner tube and filled it with fine silica sand to about two inches from the top.

"The more sand," explained Norman, "the better the insulation against vibration."

Next we fashioned tubes of various sizes to hold the optical components. These tubes were cut from black plastic waste pipe, of the kind used by plumbers, two to four inches in diameter and fourteen to eighteen inches long, with some larger ones to use as extensions. Rachel set up a card table, on which she and Arnold glued the various mirrors and lenses to corks, which were then fitted snugly into the tops of the tubes.

Norman positioned the tubes firmly in the sand, with a running commentary of what he was doing and why.

"The single ray of light from the laser will hit this partially silvered piece of glass—the beam splitter—which divides the laser beam into two. When the beam hits the glass, a small part of it will be reflected off the front surface; the amount can be adjusted by changing the angle of the glass to the light coming from the laser. This is called the reference beam, which will be spread by this lens and directed by this mirror to evenly cover the light-sensitive emulsion on the holographic plate.

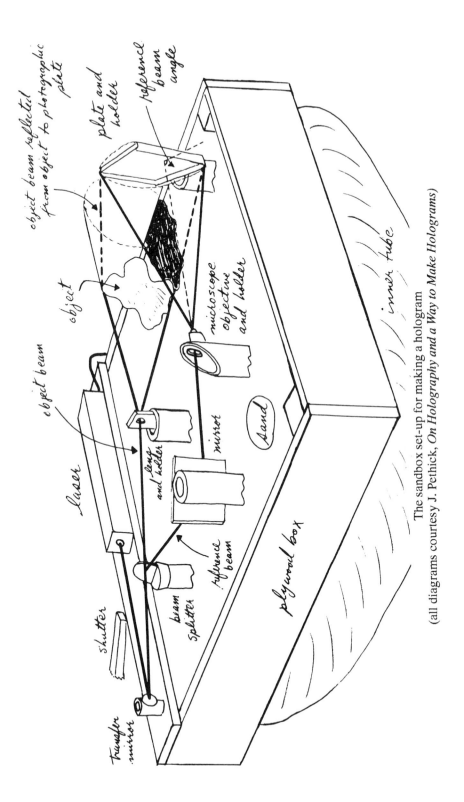

object beam reflected from object to photographic plate

plate and holder

reference beam angle

object

object beam

laser

microscope objective and holder

lens and holder

shutter

mirror

sand

beam splitter

reference beam

transfer mirror

plywood box

inner tube

The sandbox set-up for making a hologram

(all diagrams courtesy J. Pethick, *On Holography and a Way to Make Holograms*)

"The major portion of light, the object beam, will pass directly through the beam-splitting glass, striking this mirror, which will deflect the light through this lens to illuminate the object—Ms. Little— which will go here. Some of the light hitting the stone will bounce off it onto the film plate, here, thus interfering with the waves of the reference beam.

"Now, the light waves of the object beam and those making up the reference beam should travel the same distance from the beam splitter to the plate. It's also important that no light from the object beam should hit the plate directly, and no light from the reference beam should hit the object. We'll have to get it just right in order to record on the emulsion a coherent interference pattern—the visual information seen as a hologram."

When all the components were in place, Norman took Brillig's stone and rested it in the sand so the glyph side would be illuminated by the object beam from the laser. Close by it he placed a holder for the holographic plate. Then he dipped into the trunk and came up with several packets.

"In here," he said, "are a dozen glass plates. The emulsion on the film has an ASA rating of less than 1."

"That's incredible!" said Rachel. "The film I use in my camera is ASA 400."

"The lower the ASA," explained Norman, "the less grain and the better the resolution, but then you need more light to record an image. That's why we'll need an exposure of several seconds, during which everything in the sandbox must remain absolutely still."

The other packages contained standard photographic solutions for developing, fixing and washing the film. There was also a packet of bleach, with which Norman said we could get rid of the silver nitrate on the developed plate, if necessary, to improve the light transmission. That would brighten the hologram.

"Holographic plates are developed in the same way as ordinary black and white photographic film," said Norman. "The plate is exposed to the laser light in total darkness, developed for five minutes, placed in a stop bath for thirty seconds, then fixed. We'll need some basins for these solutions and also for water to rinse the plate between each stage."

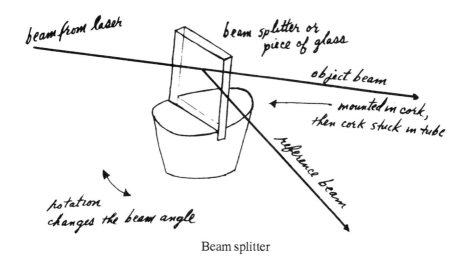

beam from laser

beam splitter or
piece of glass

object beam

mounted in cork,
then cork stuck in tube

reference beam

rotation
changes the beam angle

Beam splitter

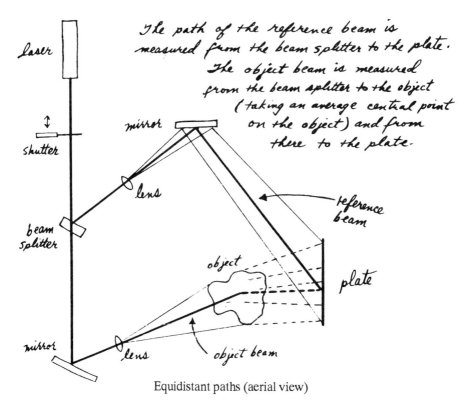

laser

shutter

mirror

lens

beam
splitter

mirror

lens

The path of the reference beam is
measured from the beam splitter to the plate.
The object beam is measured
from the beam splitter to the object
(taking an average central point
on the object) and from
there to the plate.

reference
beam

object

plate

object beam

Equidistant paths (aerial view)

While Rachel and Arnold cleared the card table and prepared the basins, Norman unpacked the laser.

It looked like nothing more than an electric pencil sharpener, only about four times as long. A thick black cable emerged from one end and there was a hole in the middle of the other.

"This is a ten-milliwatt helium-neon gas laser, emitting continuous waves of coherent red light," said Norman. "All the light waves are parallel, moving in the same direction at the same speed. It's quite adequate for illuminating a film four inches by five."

He turned it on. There was a low-pitched hum. A thin beam of red light snaked out the hole, slowly growing in intensity.

"It takes a few minutes to become stable," said Norman.

Arnold wiped his brow.

"Blows my mind," he said. "Is it like one of those death-rays in *Star Wars?*"

"Not at all," laughed Norman. "It's quite harmless, see?"—passing his hand through the beam.

It was already after five, so we took time out for a bite to eat. Arnold went upstairs and came back with glasses and a bottle of Chianti. Rachel had ordered two large pizzas—Chico's Super Extra Special Deluxe, plus double anchovies, red pepper and pineapple—which we devoured sitting on the floor in a circle. Sunny weaved among us, vacuuming up the crusts.

Arnold was exuberant.

"I haven't enjoyed myself so much since the Jays won the pennant," he grinned. "Thank you, D., for making me part of this."

He seemed to mean it.

"It really is strange," said Norman, "how the unexpected can become real."

This sounded ominously like philosophy, but he did not go on and maybe I was oversensitive.

Brillig had been pretty quiet. He was eager to help when asked, but otherwise he'd hovered in the background. Pulling strings, perhaps, though I couldn't see any. True, I did have the feeling that he was in charge, but if that were so I had to admire the way he gave us our own space.

He and Rachel were head to head. I tapped his arm.

"Hey there," I said, "how are you feeling?"

"My dear young man," chuckled Brillig. "I'm as happy as a pig in poop. This reminds me of my stint in sandplay therapy. Did you ever try it? It's amazing what you can read from the scenes people create in sand. Their psychic landscape takes shape according to the archetypal patterns constellated in the moment. Let us hope Ms. Little's will be as clear."

"Okay, folks," called Norman. "Everybody ready?"

We chorused yes.

"Lights!" cried Norman.

I pulled the switch.

Everything went dark except for the ray of red light from the laser. It was eerie. We could just make out each other's faces. Arnold was in charge of the shutter, which was simply a large block of wood he had to hold between the laser and the beam splitter until he was given the signal.

Norman inserted a glass plate in the holder.

"Now," he said quietly, activating Rachel's egg-timer. Arnold raised the shutter to allow the laser beam to do its magic. The red ray bounced off mirrors to illuminate Brillig's stone and lay a pattern of light waves on the glass plate.

Ping! went the timer—and Arnold replaced the shutter.

Norman removed the plate and plopped it in the developer. He swished it back and forth for a few minutes, then rinsed it off and dunked it in the stop-bath. After fixing and a final wash with photo-flo, Rachel blasted it with her 1200-watt hair-dryer. When it was completely dry, Norman held it at an angle in front of the laser beam. On the surface of the plate we could see a spectral smear, but the image beyond it was dull and lacked definition.

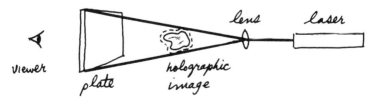

Viewing the hologram

"Visual noise," said Norman, junking it.

It took some trial and error at different exposure times, with minor adjustments of the lenses and mirrors each time. On the seventh try the image was clear, floating in space just a few inches on the other side of the plate.

"Look!" cried Rachel. "Do you see?"

"Yes, by God!" said Arnold with awe. "It's Brillig's stone, in three dimensions!"

"Not only that," said Rachel. "Move your head ... there! Do you see it?"

I was craning over their shoulders, slowly moving my head this way and that. Suddenly I saw what she meant.

Brillig's stone was only a small portion of a much larger but vaguer image.

"Holy smoke!" I shouted, while in my ears there arose that dramatic music in the film *2001,* heralding the discovery of a towering obelisk in the desert.

Brillig saw it too. He rubbed his hands.

"Mama mia!" he yelled. "The Kraznac rock!"

We linked arms and hopped around like maniacs. Sunny barked and scampered to avoid our feet.

Breathless, I broke away and turned on the lights.

Everything became still, except for the humming laser.

We looked at each other.

"I've seen that shape before," said Rachel quietly.

She searched along her bookshelf. Extracting a book she opened it to an illustration of a large rock covered with hieroglyphics. The caption described it as "a Sumerian Ur tablet."[112]

"Here," she said. "Isn't this what we just saw?"

A chill went up my spine, for indeed they looked identical.

"Let me see," said Brillig.

He took the book and leafed through it.

" 'Inanna, Queen of Heaven and Earth,' " he read. "Hmm, yes, uh-huh, hmm ... oh, goodness me, listen to this":

---

[112] See Diane Wolkstein and Samuel Noah Kramer, *Inanna, Queen of Heaven and Earth: Her Stories and Hymns,* p. 133.

Brillig's tablet

Hologram of Brillig's Kraznac tablet, with virtual image

Sumerian Ur tablet inscribed with the myth of Inanna

From the Great Above she opened her ear to the Great Below.
From the Great Above the goddess opened her ear to the Great Below.
From the Great Above Inanna opened her ear to the Great Below.[113]

"All that is above, Also is below," I recited.[114]

"Who's Inanna?" asked Norman.

"A celebrated moon goddess of the ancient world," said Rachel, "two thousand years before Christ."

Brillig read:

Female deities were worshipped and adored all through Sumerian history. . . . but the goddess who outweighed, overshadowed, and outlasted them all was a deity known to the Sumerians by the name of Inanna, "Queen of Heaven," and to the Semites who lived in Sumer by the name of Ishtar. Inanna played a greater role in myth, epic, and hymn than any other deity, male or female.[115]

"The Great Below . . ." mused Rachel.

". . . might refer to the unconscious," said Arnold.

"And the Great Above could be a metaphor for ego-consciousness," I suggested.

Brillig pursed his lips and put his palms together, as if praying.

"It's as plain as the nose on Sunny's face," he said. "What is here is also there. What is up is down. That is the essence of the psyche. The alchemists knew it, and so, apparently, did the Sumerians. But that's not the whole story.

"I should like to read you what René Daumal says about mountain climbing, which is his basic metaphor for the pursuit of self-knowledge. Norman?" He was right there. Brillig thanked him and read:

What is above knows what is below, but what is below does not know what is above. . . . There is an art of conducting oneself in the lower regions by the memory of what one saw higher up. When one can no longer see, one can at least still know.[116]

---

[113] "The Descent of Inanna," ibid., p. 52.

[114] See above, p. 9.

[115] Samuel Noah Kramer, *From the Poetry of Sumer*, p. 71 (cited in Wolkstein and Kramer, *Inanna, Queen of Heaven and Earth*, p. xv). For a psychological interpretation of the Inanna myth, see Sylvia Brinton Perera, *Descent to the Goddess: A Process of Initiation for Women.*

[116] *Mount Analogue*, p. 103.

"Daumal was a brilliant writer of allegory," said Brillig, "but not well-versed in psychology. In light of Jung's discoveries, it seems to me that we are obliged to stand Daumal's remarks on their head: *what is below knows what is above, but what is above does not know what is below.*

"Which is to say, there is an all-seeing eye in the unconscious—let us call it the Self, why not—but we puny beings, up here, can only find out what's going on down there, as the Inanna lines suggest, by listening."

"Dreams," said Arnold, "and active imagination."[117]

"Staring at the wall," I added.

"Yes," said Brillig. "And as you know, it really is an art, quite analogous to what is involved in Daumal's mountain climbing: the ability to conduct yourself consciously according to what you learn from the unconscious."

"Which one?" I teased.

"Both," he smiled. "The more we become aware of the contents of the personal unconscious—lost memories, repressed ideas and so on—the more is revealed of that rich layer of archetypal images and motifs that comprise the collective unconscious. The effect is to enlarge the personality. At least that's what Jung believed,[118] and it is also my experience."

"Mine too," I said.

"Another corollary of the Brillig Principle,"[119] noted Norman. "Whatever is experienced is true."

---

[117] A way of assimilating unconscious contents (dreams, fantasies, etc.) through some form of self-expression. See Jung, *Mysterium Coniunctionis,* CW 14, pars. 706, 753-756, and my summary in *Jung Lexicon,* pp. 12-14.

[118] Jung: "In this way there arises a consciousness which is no longer imprisoned in the petty, oversensitive, personal world of the ego, but participates freely in the wider world of objective interests. This widened consciousness is no longer that touchy, egotistical bundle of personal wishes, fears, hopes, and ambitions which always has to be compensated or corrected by unconscious counter-tendencies; instead, it is a function of relationship to the world of objects, bringing the individual into absolute, binding, and indissoluble communion with the world at large." ("The Function of the Unconscious," *Two Essays on Analytical Psychology,* CW 7, par. 275)

[119] See above, p. 37.

"Yes," agreed Brillig, "though experience is only the starting point. What really matters is what you make of it."

"Hear, hear," murmured Arnold.

"Now," said Brillig, "Jung's concept of the collective unconscious alerts us to the possibility that an archetypal image or motif that appears in one culture may also turn up in another, albeit disguised. But here, judging from the similarity between the hologram of my stone and this 'Ur tablet,' we seem to be dealing with something that has not changed at all!"

"Either that," I said slowly, "or they were one and the same to begin with."

Brillig was startled, as if this had not occurred to him.

"That bears thinking about," he nodded thoughtfully. "According to our present knowledge, the Kraznac tablets were hammered out some centuries before the Inanna rock, but clearly there is a distinct possibility that *all* the Chicken Little tablets are hitherto missing chips off the same Sumerian block."

"Gosh," said Rachel, "wouldn't that be something!—Chicken Little *is* Inanna . . ."

"Maybe just a first cousin," grinned Norman.

"All that is possible," agreed Brillig. "But let us not fly off in too many directions at once. Our immediate task is to make the most of Ms. Little—give her, and us, her due, as it were."

I eyed Brillig and suddenly realized he was dressed conservatively, in a suit and tie.

From an inside pocket he pulled a sheaf of papers.

"Gentlemen, Ms. Rachel," he said somberly, "I took the liberty of registering your names on these stock certificates in C.L. Enterprises. We each have twenty per cent."

My jaw dropped.

"I estimate that it will take six months to get it off the ground," said Brillig. "What I have in mind is a Ms. Little doll, chewing gum, tee-shirts, video games, maybe a TV series, that sort of thing."

"Yeah!" cried Arnold. "Glyphs to collect!"

I could not believe this.

"We shall of course need a book," said Brillig, "the inside story, so to speak"—and he looked at me.

"I wouldn't know where to start," I groaned.

"Listen, and it will come to you," he smiled.

Rachel nudged me.

"You do have the tools," she said.

"And the outlet," added Brillig.

I shook my head, feeling gang-banged.

"Sorry, our mandate doesn't extend to Chickle Schtick."

"Your mandate, as I understand it," said Brillig, "is self-imposed and not evangelical."

"It's not suicidal either," I replied.

Brillig picked an Inner City flyer off the sideboard, opened it and read:

> Our aim is not to convince people that a knowledge of Jungian psychology could change their lives, but rather to provide stimulating reading for those who already know that.

"You wrote this?"

I shrugged.

"All I'm suggesting," said Brillig, "is that your readers might find a mix of the two stimulating."

"Not to say bewildering," snickered Arnold.

"Thou sayest," I said, though glad to have him back.

Brillig smoothed his hair strands and pulled me aside.

"Man to man," he said, peering up at me, "I shall need to borrow Ms. Rachel."

I swallowed.

"For what purpose?"

"Research," he smiled.

Piss on you, I thought, but Rachel was already in my ear.

"Don't worry, lover," she whispered. "I'll be back."

By ten o'clock everything was packed up. We called two cabs, one for Brillig and Norman and Rachel, and one for their bags and trunks. There were hugs all around and then they were gone.

Arnold and I drove slowly back to my place, with Sunny pacing restlessly in the back. My head was awhirl. Everything had happened so fast, I didn't know what to think. It was snowing again and cars were sliding all over. We passed three accidents.

I was exhausted and felt bleak.

While I scooped out a healthy portion of Pro-Life Lite ("for older or inactive dogs"), Arnold helped himself to a glass of ice and filled it with Scotch. I boiled up some water for raspberry tea.

"Well?" said Arnold.

"Well yourself," I grumped.

Silence.

"It's a fair cop," said Arnold. "She's in safe hands."

"Yeah? What about me?"

"As it happens, I have some ideas . . ."

Well, Arnold is nothing if not inventive. His suggestions would certainly disturb my life, but on the other hand they might enhance it as well. I felt more than a spark of interest. Being outside hadn't been so bad after all. I learned something new, and I still felt me. I wasn't happy that Rachel was gone, but you don't lose somebody like her just because she's not beside you.

"I'll have to sleep on it," I said cautiously.

But meanwhile there was this Chicken Little business to wrap up. Was Brillig on to something important? Was the whole idea just a flash in the pan, another dead end? Was it worth pursuing?

After staring at the wall for a few days, I realized that my questions were academic. I knew where my energy wanted to go. Like Ms. Little, believed or not, I had to speak out. That was my destiny.

I sat down at the computer and made a tentative start.

I got back from the bank just as Rachel was pulling out. She rolled down her window.

"Sunny hasn't had her walk," she called. "Oh, and there's a special delivery letter on your desk. Don't know who it's from, I didn't open it. Gotta fly!"

And she blew me a kiss, off to her class.

"Yeah!" said Arnold. "Do it."

And I did.

Epilogue

I have been asked to say a few words. I would be glad to oblige had not an accident of birth rendered me incapable of speech. However, I presume writing will do, as this is not a recording; if it were, I would have to decline the invitation. Thanks, but no thanks, I'd "say."

The main thing I'm thinking is that maybe I'll get more walks now that this is finished. All that talk about neglected chickens and stones, but what about me? Sniffing is my life and I haven't had enough. Maybe they think a stroll around the swimming pool in D.'s dinky back yard is enough; well, it's not. So Ms. Rachel meets some interesting people in the park? That's gravy in her life; their dogs are all I've got.

Don't get me wrong. I have no quarrel at all with Ms. Little. Sure, I've chased a few of her kind, but who hasn't? If I could be born again, I wouldn't mind at all coming back as one. I might learn to fly. But you know what? This "Who am I" question takes the cake. Maybe that's what happens when you live too much in your head— you forget who you are. I mean I know already, I don't have to ask.

As for that ditsy professor, I could out-philosophize him any day. Consider this:

> One day a god happened to think of Man, just a fleeting thought, a bare hint of the possibilities, gone even before the god himself was fully aware of what had crossed his mind. But that instant, in the life of an ageless god who exists through all eternity, represented a thousand million years of life on earth, during which time Man crawled out of the sea, came down from the trees, evolved a mind, progressed in science and the arts, reached out to the stars, and would have usurped the authority of the god himself, had it not been such a fleeting thought.

Now I ask you, what if that god had happened to think of Dog instead?

See you in the park.

Bibliography

Birkhäuser-Oeri, Sibylle. *The Mother: Archetypal Image in Fairy Tales.* Toronto: Inner City Books, 1988.

Carroll, Lewis. *Through the Looking Glass, and What Alice Found There.* New York: St. Martin's Press, 1968.

Céline, Louis-Ferdinand. *Journey to the End of the Night.* New York: New Directions, 1983.

Chambers, Carole. *Still Life Under the Occupation.* Toronto: Quadrant Editions, 1988.

Dostoyevsky, Fyodor. *Notes from Underground.* Trans. Andrew McAndrew. New York: Signet, 1961.

Edinger, Edward F. *Anatomy of the Psyche: Alchemical Symbolism in Psychotherapy.* La Sale, IL: Open Court, 1985.

_____. *The Creation of Consciousness: Jung's Myth for Modern Man.* Toronto: Inner City Books, 1984.

_____. *Transformation of the God-Image: An Elucidation of Jung's Answer to Job.* Toronto: Inner City Books, 1992.

Ellenberger, Henri F. *The Discovery of the Unconscious: The History and Evolution of Dynamic Psychiatry.* New York: Basic Books, 1970.

Hall, James A. *Jungian Dream Interpretation: A Handbook of Theory and Practice.* Toronto: Inner City Books, 1983.

Harding, M. Esther. *Woman's Mysteries: Ancient and Modern.* New York: Bantam Books, 1973.

Hollis, James. *The Middle Passage: From Misery to Meaning in Midlife.* Toronto: Inner City Books, 1993.

Huxley. Aldous. *Doors of Perception, and Heaven and Hell.* New York: Harper and Row, 1956.

Jackson, Graham. *The Secret Lore of Gardening: Patterns of Male Intimacy.* Toronto: Inner City Books, 1991.

Jung, C.G. *The Collected Works* (Bollingen Series XX), 20 vols. Trans. R.F.C. Hull. Ed. H. Read, M. Fordham, G. Adler, Wm. McGuire. Princeton: Princeton University Press, 1953-1979.

_____. *Letters* (Bollingen Series XCV). 2 vols. Ed. Gerhard Adler and Aniela Jaffé. Princeton: Princeton University Press, 1973.

_____. *Memories, Dreams, Reflections.* Ed. Aniela Jaffé. New York: Pantheon Books, 1961.

Kafka, Franz. *The Diaries of Franz Kafka, 1910-1913.* Trans. Joseph Kresh. Ed. Max Brod. London: Secker & Warburg, 1948.

_____. *The Diaries of Franz Kafka, 1914-1923.* Trans. Martin Greenberg. Ed. Max Brod. London: Secker & Warburg, 1949.

Kierkegaard, Soren. *The Journals of Kierkegaard, 1834-1854.* Trans. and ed. Alexander Dru. London: Fontana Books, 1958.

Kramer, Samuel Noah. *From the Poetry of Sumer.* Berkeley: University of Berkeley Press, 1979.

Lawrence, D.H. *Phoenix: The Posthumous Papers of D.H. Lawrence.* London, Heinemann, 1936.

McNeely, Deldon Anne. *Touching: Body Therapy and Depth Psychology.* Toronto: Inner City Books, 1987.

McPherson, Sigrid. *The Refiner's Fire: Memoirs of a German Girlhood.* Toronto: Inner City Books, 1992.

Nietzsche, Friedrich. *The Portable Nietzsche.* Trans. and ed. Walter Kaufmann. New York: The Viking Press, 1954.

Perera, Sylvia Brinton. *Descent to the Goddess: A Way of Initiation for Women.* Toronto: Inner City Books, 1981.

Pethick, J. *On Holography and a Way To Make Holograms.* Burlington, ON: Belltower Enterprises, 1971 (out of print).

Rilke, Rainer Maria. *The Notebook of Malte Laurids Brigge.* Trans. John Linton. London: The Hogarth Press, 1959.

Sanford, John. *The Man Who Wrestled with God.* King of Prussia, PA: Religious Publishing Co., 1976.

Schapira, Laurie Layton. *The Cassandra Complex: Living with Disbelief.* Toronto: Inner City Books, 1988.

Sharp, Daryl. *Dear Gladys: The Survival Papers, Books 2.* Toronto: Inner City Books, 1989

_____. *Getting To Know You: The Inside Out of Relationship.* Toronto: Inner City Books, 1992.

_____. *Jung Lexicon: A Primer of Terms and Concepts.* Toronto: Inner City Books, 1991.

_____. *Personality Types: Jung's Model of Typology.* Toronto: Inner City Books, 1987.

_____. *The Secret Raven: Conflict and Transformation in the Life of Franz Kafka.* Toronto: Inner City Books, 1980.

_____. *The Survival Papers: Anatomy of a Midlife Crisis.* Toronto: Inner City Books, 1988.

von Franz, Marie-Louise. *Alchemy: An Introduction to the Symbolism and the Psychology.* Toronto: Inner City Books, 1980.

_____. *Puer Aeternus: A Psychological Study of the Adult Struggle with the Paradise of Childhood.* 2nd ed. Santa Monica, CA: Sigo Press, 1981.

Wolkstein, Diane, and Kramer, Samuel Noah. *Inanna, Queen of Heaven and Earth: Her Stories and Hymns.* New York: Harper and Row, 1983.

Woodman, Marion. *Addiction to Perfection: The Still Unravished Bride.* Toronto: Inner City Books, 1982.

_____. *The Owl Was a Baker's Daughter: Obesity, Anorexia Nervosa and the Repressed Feminine.* Toronto: Inner City Books, 1980.

_____. *The Pregnant Virgin: A Process of Psychological Transformation.* Toronto: Inner City Books, 1985.

Studies in Jungian Psychology
by Jungian Analysts

Quality Paperbacks

Prices and payment in $U.S. (in Canada, $Cdn)

1. The Secret Raven: Conflict and Transformation
Daryl Sharp (Toronto). ISBN 0-919123-00-7. 128 pp. $15

2. The Psychological Meaning of Redemption Motifs in Fairy Tales
Marie-Louise von Franz (Zurich). ISBN 0-919123-01-5. 128 pp. $15

3. On Divination and Synchronicity: The Psychology of Meaningful Chance   Marie-Louise von Franz (Zurich). ISBN 0-919123-02-3. 128 pp. $15

4. The Owl Was a Baker's Daughter: Obesity, Anorexia Nervosa and the Repressed Feminine
Marion Woodman (Toronto). ISBN 0-919123-03-1. 144 pp. $16

5. Alchemy: An Introduction to the Symbolism and the Psychology
Marie-Louise von Franz (Zurich). ISBN 0-919123-04-X. 288 pp. $18

6. Descent to the Goddess: A Way of Initiation for Women
Sylvia Brinton Perera (New York). ISBN 0-919123-05-8. 112 pp. $15

7. The Psyche as Sacrament: A Comparative Study of C.G. Jung and Paul Tillich
John P. Dourley (Ottawa). ISBN 0-919123-06-6. 128 pp. $15

8. Border Crossings: Carlos Castaneda's Path of Knowledge
Donald Lee Williams (Boulder). ISBN 0-919123-07-4. 160 pp. $16

9. Narcissism and Character Transformation: The Psychology of Narcissistic Character Disorders
Nathan Schwartz-Salant (New York). ISBN 0-919123-08-2. 192 pp. $18

10. Rape and Ritual: A Psychological Study
Bradley A. Te Paske (Minneapolis). ISBN 0-919123-09-0. 160 pp. $16

11. Alcoholism and Women: The Background and the Psychology
Jan Bauer (Montreal). ISBN 0-919123-10-4. 144 pp. $16

12. Addiction to Perfection: The Still Unravished Bride
Marion Woodman (Toronto). ISBN 0-919123-11-2. 208 pp. $18pb/$20hc

13. Jungian Dream Interpretation: A Handbook of Theory and Practice
James A. Hall, M.D. (Dallas). ISBN 0-919123-12-0. 128 pp. $15

14. The Creation of Consciousness: Jung's Myth for Modern Man
Edward F. Edinger (Los Angeles). ISBN 0-919123-13-9. 128 pp. $15

15. The Analytic Encounter: Transference and Human Relationship
Mario Jacoby (Zurich). ISBN 0-919123-14-7. 128 pp. $15

16. Change of Life: Dreams and the Menopause5
Ann Mankowitz (Santa Fe). ISBN 0-919123-15-5. 128 pp. $15

17. The Illness That We Are: A Jungian Critique of Christianity
John P. Dourley (Ottawa). ISBN 0-919123-16-3. 128 pp. $15

18. Hags and Heroes: A Feminist Approach to Jungian Psychotherapy with Couples
Polly Young-Eisendrath (Philadelphia). ISBN 0-919123-17-1. 192 pp. $18

Add Postage/Handling: 1-2 books, $2; 3-4 books, $4; 5-8 books, $7

INNER CITY BOOKS   Tel. 416-927-0355
Box 1271, Station Q, Toronto, ON, Canada M4T 2P4